Billbc

TOP 1

SINGLES

1955 2000

Portions of the *Billboard* chart material in this work were constructed
from information provided by Broadcast Data Systems (BDS), which
actual radio airplay, and Soundscan, Inc., which electronically c
information from music retail outlets.

HAL•LEONARD®
CORPORATION

7777 W. BLUEMOUND RD. P.O. BOX 13819 MILWAUKEE, WI 53213

CONTENTS

JANUARY 1, 1955 — DECEMBER 30, 2000

A ranking of the Top 1000 hits compiled from Billboard magazine's pop singles charts.

Year-by-year rankings of each year's 40 biggest hits.

Color photos of the Top 100 Albums compiled from Billboard magazine's pop albums charts.

An alphabetical listing, by artist name, of the Top 1000 hits.

An alphabetical listing, by song title, of the Top 1000 hits.

AUTHOR'S NOTE

What's in? What's out? Who's hot? Who's not? This common fascination with the latest and the greatest is ever promoted with an abundance of awards shows, Top 10 lists, critics' ratings, and audience polls.

The longest-running popular song contests are found in the pages of *Billboard* magazine. The charts within each weekly issue chronicle the hottest music of the moment based on sales and radio airplay success. Earning a spot on the charts is a hallmark of mainstream musical achievement.

The highest chart honor is the spot at #1. All songs that have topped *Billboard*'s pop singles charts since the dawn of the rock era are in the Top 1000 ranking. In addition to every #1 hit, it includes the runners-up at #2 that spent the most weeks challenging the coveted throne.

Beyond the Top 1000 ranking, this book includes even more hit songs plus the biggest hit albums. The year-by-year lists of the 40 most popular songs of each year, from 1955 through 2000, include hits which do not appear in the Top 1000 ranking. The Top 100 albums since 1955 are displayed in the color photo section.

Top 1000 spans four-and-a-half decades of pop music. So, whether the mention of a popular female singer/actress immediately brings to mind Doris Day, Shelley Fabares or Jennifer Lopez, you'll find the popular music of your favorite era well represented in this ranking.

Joel Whitburn

THE RANKING SYSTEM

All chart data is compiled from *Billboard* magazine's pop singles charts. See the synopsis below for a breakdown of those charts.

Our ranking methodology is based on the most-quoted of all chart statistics, the peak position. Basically, the peak position of a song title and the weeks it held that position determine its final ranking.

Following is the ranking formula:

1) All songs that peaked at #1 are listed first, followed by songs that peaked at #2, and so on.
2) Ties among these #1 (and #2) songs are broken down in the following order:
   a) Total weeks at the peak position
   b) Total weeks in the Top 10
   c) Total weeks in the Top 40
   d) Total weeks charted

If ties still existed, a computerized inverse point system calculated a point total for each song based on its weekly chart positions. For each week that a song appeared on the charts, it earned points according to each of its weekly chart positions (#1=100, #2=99 points, etc.). The sum of these points broke any remaining ties.

Below is a synopsis of *Billboard* magazine's pop singles charts, researched from the first year of the rock era, 1955. For a song that appeared on more than one of the multiple weekly charts (Juke Box, Best Sellers, Jockeys or Top 100), its peak position is determined by the chart on which it achieved its highest peak.

DATE	CHART	POSITIONS
1/1/55– 6/17/57 (final chart)	MOST PLAYED IN JUKE BOXES	15-30
1/1/55– 10/13/58 (final chart)	BEST SELLERS IN STORES	20-50
1/1/55– 7/28/58 (final chart)	MOST PLAYED BY JOCKEYS	15-30
11/12/55– 7/28/58 (final chart)	TOP 100	100
8/4/58 (first chart)	HOT 100 First, all-encompassing chart.	100
11/30/91	HOT 100 *Billboard* begins using actual monitored airplay (from Broadcast DataSystems), actual sales figures (from SoundScan) and playlists from small-market radio stations to compile the chart.	100
12/5/98	HOT 100 Billboard begins to include airplay hits that are not commercially available as singles.	100

THE RANKING

These are the Top 1000 hits compiled from *Billboard* magazine's pop singles charts from January 1, 1955 through December 30, 2000. February 10, 2001 is the research cut-off date for three hits that were still on the "Hot 100": "Independent Women Part 1," "With Arms Wide Open" and "Case Of The Ex (Whatcha Gonna Do)." For these hits, their peak weeks are final, but, their total weeks in the Top 10, Top 40 and weeks charted will be greater than listed within.

The beginning and ending rank numbers of each page are listed on the upper outside corner of the page.

Keep track of the Top 1000 hits in your collection by checking off the small circle in front of the titles.

> **1**[5] The **PEAK POSITION** and the **PEAK WEEKS** (total weeks at peak position) are highlighted above the corresponding titles.

Columnar headings show the following data:

YR: Year title reached its peak position

WEEKS: **10** - Total weeks charted in the Top 10
 40 - Total weeks charted in the Top 40
 CH - Total weeks charted

RANK: Top 1000 ranking (highlighted in dark type)

GOLD: ● - RIAA-certified gold single
 ▲ - RIAA-certified platinum single (a number following the triangle indicates additional million units sold)

The Recording Industry Association of America (RIAA) began certifying gold singles in 1958 and platinum singles in 1976. From 1958 through 1988, RIAA required sales of one million units for a gold single and two million units for a platinum single. As of January 1, 1989, RIAA lowered the certification requirements for gold singles to sales of 500,000 units and for platinum to one million units. Some record companies have never requested RIAA certifications for their hits. To fill in the gaps prior to 1958, other trade publications and reports were consulted.

SYM (Symbol for type of recording):
 [F] Foreign language [S] Spoken word [R] Re-entry, reissue,
 [I] Instrumental [X] Christmas remix or re-recording or
 [N] Novelty a prior hit by the artist

TIME: Playing time of each song

YR	WEEKS			RANK	G O L D	PEAK POSITION	PEAK WEEKS	S Y M	TIME	ARTIST
	CH	40	10							
						Pos 1 16 Wks				
95	27	26	19	1	O	▲² One Sweet Day..................			4:42	Mariah Carey & Boyz II Men
						Pos 1 14 Wks				
96	60	37	23	2	O	▲⁴ Macarena (bayside boys mix)	[F]		3:54	Los Del Rio
94	33	31	22	3	O	▲ I'll Make Love To You			3:58	Boyz II Men
97	42	28	17	4	O	▲¹¹ Candle In The Wind 1997 / Something About The Way You Look Tonight	[R]		4:08 / 3:57	Elton John
92	26	24	16	5	O	▲⁴ I Will Always Love You			4:32	Whitney Houston
						Pos 1 13 Wks				
92	32	28	19	6	O	▲ End of the Road..................			5:50	Boyz II Men
98	27	27	18	7	O	▲² The Boy Is Mine			4:00	Brandy & Monica
						Pos 1 12 Wks				
99	58	50	30	8	O	▲ Smooth........................			4:04	Santana Feat. Rob Thomas
						Pos 1 11 Wks				
96	42	37	25	9	O	▲ Un-Break My Heart................			4:24	Toni Braxton
56	27	23	21	10	O	▲⁴ Don't Be Cruel / Hound Dog			2:03 / 2:15	Elvis Presley
94	30	26	18	11	O	▲ I Swear			4:15	All-4-One
97	33	29	17	12	O	▲³ I'll Be Missing You			5:02	Puff Daddy & Faith Evans (Feat. 112)
00	21+	18+	15+	13	O	Independent Women Part 1			3:38	Destiny's Child
						Pos 1 10 Wks				
55	26	26	20	14	O	● Cherry Pink And Apple Blossom White	[I]		2:56	Perez Prado
00	26	24	18	15	O	▲ Maria Maria.....................			4:18	Santana Featuring The Product G&B
55	21	21	18	16	O	● Sincerely			2:54	The McGuire Sisters
56	26	22	17	17	O	● Singing The Blues			2:23	Guy Mitchell
81	26	21	15	18	O	▲ Physical			3:43	Olivia Newton-John
77	25	21	14	19	O	▲ You Light Up My Life			3:35	Debby Boone
						Pos 1 9 Wks				
59	26	22	16	20	O	● Mack The Knife...................			3:04	Bobby Darin
57	30	22	15	21	O	▲² All Shook Up			1:58	Elvis Presley
81	26	20	14	22	O	● Bette Davis Eyes			3:47	Kim Carnes
68	19	19	14	23	O	▲⁴ Hey Jude			7:11	The Beatles
81	27	19	13	24	O	▲ Endless Love			4:26	Diana Ross & Lionel Richie
60	21	17	12	25	O	● The Theme From "A Summer Place". .	[I]		2:24	Percy Faith
						Pos 1 8 Wks				
55	38	25	19	26	O	● (We're Gonna) Rock Around The Clock. .			2:08	Bill Haley & His Comets
95	25	23	16	27	O	▲² Fantasy.......................			4:03	Mariah Carey
56	37	22	16	28	O	● The Wayward Wind................			2:56	Gogi Grant

YR	WEEKS			RANK	GOLD	PEAK POSITION	PEAK WEEKS	SYM	TIME	ARTIST
	CH	40	10							

Pos 1 — 8 Wks Cont'd

YR	CH	40	10	RANK	GOLD	PEAK POSITION	TIME	ARTIST
55	22	19	16	29	O ●	Sixteen Tons	2:34	"Tennessee" Ernie Ford
56	27	22	15	30	O ▲²	Heartbreak Hotel	2:06	Elvis Presley
93	29	26	14	31	O ▲	Dreamlover	3:53	Mariah Carey
93	23	20	14	32	O ▲	That's The Way Love Goes	4:27	Janet Jackson
83	22	20	13	33	O ●	Every Breath You Take	4:13	The Police
92	21	18	13	34	O ▲²	Jump	3:12	Kris Kross
78	20	18	13	35	O ▲	Night Fever	3:32	Bee Gees
96	20	16	12	36	O ▲²	Tha Crossroads	3:48	Bone thugs-n-harmony
76	23	17	11	37	O ●	Tonight's The Night (Gonna Be Alright)	3:55	Rod Stewart

Pos 1 — 7 Wks

YR	CH	40	10	RANK	GOLD	PEAK POSITION	TIME	ARTIST
95	34	28	18	38	O ▲	Waterfalls	4:09	TLC
57	34	24	17	39	O ●	Love Letters In The Sand	2:12	Pat Boone
95	30	27	15	40	O ●	Take A Bow	5:13	Madonna
93	29	23	15	41	O ▲	Can't Help Falling In Love	3:18	UB40
57	27	19	15	42	O ▲²	Jailhouse Rock	2:10	Elvis Presley
95	29	24	14	43	O ▲	This Is How We Do It	3:56	Montell Jordan
57	25	18	14	44	O ▲²	(Let Me Be Your) Teddy Bear	1:43	Elvis Presley
93	25	19	13	45	O ▲	Informer	4:05	Snow
78	25	19	12	46	O ▲	Shadow Dancing	4:32	Andy Gibb
58	21	18	12	47	O ●	At The Hop	2:31	Danny & The Juniors
61	23	17	12	48	O	Tossin' And Turnin'	2:40	Bobby Lewis
82	20	16	12	49	O ▲	I Love Rock 'N' Roll	2:45	Joan Jett & The Blackhearts
82	19	15	12	50	O ●	Ebony And Ivory	3:41	Paul McCartney (with Stevie Wonder)
64	15	14	12	51	O ●	I Want To Hold Your Hand	2:24	The Beatles
66	15	13	12	52	O ●	I'm A Believer	2:41	The Monkees
83	24	17	11	53	O ▲	Billie Jean	4:50	Michael Jackson
68	15	15	11	54	O	I Heard It Through The Grapevine	2:59	Marvin Gaye
91	22	17	10	55	O ▲³	(Everything I Do) I Do It For You	4:03	Bryan Adams
91	20	15	10	56	O ▲	Black Or White	3:19	Michael Jackson

Pos 1 — 6 Wks

YR	CH	40	10	RANK	GOLD	PEAK POSITION	TIME	ARTIST
94	41	33	21	57	O ▲	The Sign	3:10	Ace Of Base
96	33	30	19	58	O ▲	Because You Loved Me	4:23	Celine Dion
94	27	25	17	59	O ▲	On Bended Knee	5:25	Boyz II Men
55	21	21	17	60	O ●	Love Is A Many-Splendored Thing	2:56	Four Aces
97	28	26	16	61	O ▲²	Can't Nobody Hold Me Down	4:53	Puff Daddy Featuring Ma$e
56	25	20	16	62	O ●	Rock And Roll Waltz	2:53	Kay Starr
56	24	20	16	63	O ●	The Poor People Of Paris [I]	2:24	Les Baxter
55	19	19	16	64	O ●	The Yellow Rose Of Texas	3:00	Mitch Miller
78	25	19	15	65	O ▲	Le Freak	3:30	Chic
56	24	19	15	66	O ●	Memories Are Made Of This	2:15	Dean Martin
82	25	18	15	67	O ▲²	Eye Of The Tiger	3:45	Survivor
83	25	20	14	68	O ●	Flashdance...What A Feeling	3:55	Irene Cara
57	26	19	14	69	O ●	April Love	2:39	Pat Boone
80	25	19	13	70	O ●	Lady	3:51	Kenny Rogers
83	22	18	13	71	O ▲	Say Say Say	3:55	Paul McCartney/ Michael Jackson
59	21	18	13	72	O ●	The Battle Of New Orleans	2:33	Johnny Horton
57	21	17	13	73	O ●	Young Love	2:24	Tab Hunter

YR	CH	40	10	RANK	G O L D	PEAK POSITION	PEAK WEEKS	S Y M	TIME	ARTIST
						Pos 1 6 Wks Cont'd				
82	25	20	12	74	O ●	Centerfold			3:35	The J. Geils Band
80	25	19	12	75	O ●	Call Me			3:30	Blondie
58	22	19	12	76	O ●	It's All In The Game			2:25	Tommy Edwards
79	26	16	12	77	O ●	My Sharona			3:58	The Knack
69	17	16	11	78	O ▲	Aquarius/Let The Sunshine In (The Flesh Failures)			4:45	The 5th Dimension
72	18	15	11	79	O ●	The First Time Ever I Saw Your Face			4:15	Roberta Flack
72	18	15	11	80	O ●	Alone Again (Naturally)			3:40	Gilbert O'Sullivan
71	17	15	11	81	O ●	Joy To The World			3:17	Three Dog Night
60	16	14	11	82	O ▲²	Are You Lonesome To-night?			3:07	Elvis Presley
98	18	15	10	83	O ▲	I'm Your Angel			5:31	R. Kelly & Celine Dion
58	14	14	10	84	O ●	The Purple People Eater		[N]	2:11	Sheb Wooley
70	14	13	10	85	O ●	Bridge Over Troubled Water			4:55	Simon & Garfunkel
84	19	14	9	86	O ●	Like A Virgin			3:35	Madonna
69	13	12	9	87	O ●	In The Year 2525 (Exordium & Terminus)			3:15	Zager & Evans
						Pos 1 5 Wks				
98	53	49	23	88	O ▲	Too Close			4:07	Next
57	31	23	16	89	O ●	Tammy			3:00	Debbie Reynolds
98	23	23	16	90	O ▲	The First Night			3:53	Monica
55	20	20	16	91	O ●	The Ballad Of Davy Crockett			2:20	Bill Hayes
92	28	24	15	92	O ▲²	Baby Got Back			4:24	Sir Mix-A-Lot
99	25	20	15	93	O ▲	If You Had My Love			4:25	Jennifer Lopez
56	23	19	15	94	O ▲³	Love Me Tender			2:42	Elvis Presley
99	25	23	14	95	O ▲	Genie In A Bottle			3:36	Christina Aguilera
56	23	20	14	96	O ●	My Prayer			2:45	The Platters
80	22	19	14	97	O ●	(Just Like) Starting Over			3:54	John Lennon
93	22	18	14	98	O ▲	I'd Do Anything For Love (But I Won't Do That)			5:08	Meat Loaf
99	20	17	14	99	O ▲	Livin' La Vida Loca			4:03	Ricky Martin
92	27	23	13	100	O ●	Save The Best For Last			3:39	Vanessa Williams
95	24	20	12	101	O	Have You Ever Really Loved A Woman?			4:45	Bryan Adams
77	23	17	12	102	O ●	Best Of My Love			3:40	Emotions
58	19	16	12	103	O ●	All I Have To Do Is Dream			2:17	The Everly Brothers
84	21	16	11	104	O ▲	When Doves Cry			3:49	Prince
60	20	16	11	105	O ▲	It's Now Or Never			3:12	Elvis Presley
58	19	16	11	106	O ●	Tequila		[I]	2:09	The Champs
70	16	16	11	107	O	I'll Be There			3:44	The Jackson 5
76	19	15	11	108	O ●	Silly Love Songs			5:54	Wings
71	17	15	11	109	O ●	Maggie May			5:15	Rod Stewart
62	18	14	11	110	O ●	I Can't Stop Loving You			2:37	Ray Charles
58	20	16	10	111	O ▲	Don't			2:48	Elvis Presley
84	21	15	10	112	O ●	Jump			4:04	Van Halen
79	20	15	10	113	O ▲	Bad Girls			3:55	Donna Summer
68	18	15	10	114	O ●	Love Is Blue		[I]	2:31	Paul Mauriat
71	17	15	10	115	O ●	It's Too Late			3:51	Carole King
59	17	14	10	116	O ●	Venus			2:21	Frankie Avalon

YR	WEEKS			RANK	G O L D		PEAK POSITION	PEAK WEEKS	S Y M	TIME	ARTIST
	CH	40	10								

Pos 1 5 Wks Cont'd

YR	CH	40	10	RANK	GOLD		TITLE		TIME	ARTIST
62	16	14	10	117	O	●	Big Girls Don't Cry..................		2:25	The 4 Seasons
58	16	13	10	118	O	●	Nel Blu Dipinto Di Blu (Volaré) .... [F]		3:29	Domenico Modugno
61	16	13	10	119	O	●	Big Bad John................... [S]		2:57	Jimmy Dean
63	15	13	10	120	O	●	Sugar Shack.....................		2:01	Jimmy Gilmer & The Fireballs
68	15	13	10	121	O	●	Honey.........................		3:58	Bobby Goldsboro
91	19	15	9	122	O	●	Rush, Rush		4:14	Paula Abdul
67	17	15	9	123	O	●	To Sir With Love.................		2:44	Lulu
60	17	13	9	124	O	●	Cathy's Clown		2:22	The Everly Brothers
73	16	13	9	125	O	●	Killing Me Softly With His Song		4:46	Roberta Flack
68	14	13	9	126	O	●	People Got To Be Free.............		2:57	The Rascals
71	15	12	9	127	O	●	One Bad Apple...................		2:45	The Osmonds
69	12	12	9	128	O	▲²	Get Back......................		3:08	The Beatles with Billy Preston
66	13	11	9	129	O	●	The Ballad Of The Green Berets		2:27	SSgt Barry Sadler
62	14	12	7	130	O	●	Sherry.......................		2:07	The 4 Seasons
64	10	9	6	131	O	●	Can't Buy Me Love..............		2:12	The Beatles

Pos 1 4 Wks

YR	CH	40	10	RANK	GOLD		TITLE		TIME	ARTIST
95	32	29	20	132	O	▲	Creep		4:21	TLC
96	31	26	18	133	O	▲	No Diggity		5:10	BLACKstreet (Featuring Dr. Dre)
55	26	26	18	134	O	●	Autumn Leaves................. [I]		2:52	Roger Williams
00	33	28	17	135	O	●	I Knew I Loved You...............		4:07	Savage Garden
99	28	25	17	136	O	●	No Scrubs		3:39	TLC
56	29	24	17	137	O	●	Lisbon Antigua .... [I]		2:33	Nelson Riddle
94	33	26	16	138	O	▲	The Power Of Love		4:46	Celine Dion
99	31	25	16	139	O	▲	Believe		3:59	Cher
93	30	25	16	140	O	▲	Hero		4:17	Mariah Carey
77	31	23	16	141	O	●	I Just Want To Be Your Everything....		3:32	Andy Gibb
99	30	26	15	142	O	●	Angel Of Mine		4:10	Monica
97	23	22	15	143	O	▲	Wannabe		2:50	Spice Girls
56	23	19	14	144	O	●	I Almost Lost My Mind..............		2:27	Pat Boone
80	29	17	14	145	O	●	Upside Down		3:37	Diana Ross
57	28	23	13	146	O	●	Honeycomb		2:14	Jimmie Rodgers
78	27	22	13	147	O	▲	Stayin' Alive		3:41	Bee Gees
70	22	19	13	148	O	●	Raindrops Keep Fallin' On My Head ...		3:02	B.J. Thomas
83	24	17	13	149	O	●	All Night Long (All Night)		4:16	Lionel Richie
82	23	17	13	150	O	●	Maneater		4:30	Daryl Hall & John Oates
94	25	23	12	151	O	▲	Bump N' Grind		4:07	R. Kelly
00	24	22	12	152	O	▲	Music		3:45	Madonna
57	26	20	12	153	O	●	Wake Up Little Susie		1:57	The Everly Brothers
80	25	19	12	154	O	●	Another Brick In The Wall (Part II)		3:10	Pink Floyd
58	23	19	12	155	O	●	Sugartime.....................		2:29	The McGuire Sisters
69	22	18	12	156	O	●	Sugar, Sugar		2:48	The Archies
79	21	18	12	157	O	▲	Da Ya Think I'm Sexy?		5:21	Rod Stewart
78	23	17	12	158	O	●	Kiss You All Over		3:30	Exile
80	22	17	12	159	O	●	Crazy Little Thing Called Love.......		2:44	Queen
55	16	16	12	160	O	●	Let Me Go Lover		2:20	Joan Weber
83	29	18	11	161	O	●	Total Eclipse Of The Heart.........		4:29	Bonnie Tyler
73	23	17	11	162	O	●	Tie A Yellow Ribbon Round The Ole Oak Tree		3:19	Dawn Featuring Tony Orlando
72	19	17	11	163	O	●	American Pie - Parts I & II...........		8:36	Don McLean
70	17	15	11	164	O	●	(They Long To Be) Close To You		3:40	Carpenters

YR	CH	40	10	RANK	GOLD	PEAK POSITION	PEAK WEEKS	SYM	TIME	ARTIST
						Pos **1** **4** Wks Cont'd				
68	16	14	11	165	O	● (Sittin' On) The Dock Of The Bay			2:38	Otis Redding
69	15	14	11	166	O	● Honky Tonk Women			3:03	The Rolling Stones
83	25	19	10	167	O	● Down Under			3:41	Men At Work
86	23	17	10	168	O	● That's What Friends Are For			3:58	Dionne & Friends
82	22	17	10	169	O	● Jack & Diane			4:16	John Cougar
90	23	16	10	170	O	● Because I Love You (The Postman Song)			4:15	Stevie B
79	23	15	10	171	O	▲ Reunited			3:58	Peaches & Herb
90	21	15	10	172	O	▲ Nothing Compares 2 U			5:09	Sinéad O'Connor
59	21	15	10	173	O	● Stagger Lee			2:20	Lloyd Price
98	20	14	10	174	O	● I Don't Want To Miss A Thing			4:50	Aerosmith
89	18	14	10	175	O	● Another Day In Paradise			4:48	Phil Collins
59	17	14	10	176	O	● The Three Bells			2:47	The Browns
59	15	14	10	177	O	● Lonely Boy			2:33	Paul Anka
71	15	14	10	178	O	● How Can You Mend A Broken Heart			3:52	The Bee Gees
60	16	13	10	179	O	● Stuck On You			2:17	Elvis Presley
62	15	13	10	180	O	● Roses Are Red (My Love)			2:37	Bobby Vinton
70	14	13	10	181	O	● My Sweet Lord			4:39	George Harrison
67	16	12	10	182	O	● Daydream Believer			2:57	The Monkees
80	24	19	9	183	O	▲ Rock With You			3:20	Michael Jackson
80	23	16	9	184	O	● Magic			4:25	Olivia Newton-John
85	20	16	9	185	O	● Say You, Say Me			3:59	Lionel Richie
80	23	15	9	186	O	▲ Funkytown			3:57	Lipps, Inc.
87	20	15	9	187	O	● Faith			3:14	George Michael
73	18	15	9	188	O	● My Love			4:07	Paul McCartney/Wings
69	19	14	9	189	O	● Everyday People			2:18	Sly & The Family Stone
72	19	14	9	190	O	● Without You			3:16	Nilsson
58	19	14	9	191	O	● He's Got The Whole World (In His Hands)			2:20	Laurie London
69	15	13	9	192	O	● Dizzy			2:55	Tommy Roe
67	14	13	9	193	O	● Windy			2:49	The Association
67	20	12	9	194	O	● Ode To Billie Joe			4:13	Bobbie Gentry
61	17	12	9	195	O	● Runaway			2:20	Del Shannon
63	15	12	9	196	O	He's So Fine			1:53	The Chiffons
65	14	12	9	197	O	● (I Can't Get No) Satisfaction			3:45	The Rolling Stones
63	13	12	9	198	O	Dominique	[F]		2:53	The Singing Nun
64	13	12	9	199	O	There! I've Said It Again			2:20	Bobby Vinton
67	13	11	9	200	O	● Somethin' Stupid			2:35	Nancy Sinatra & Frank Sinatra
67	13	11	9	201	O	● Groovin'			2:25	The Young Rascals
00	21	16	8	202	O	● Come On Over Baby (all I want is you)			3:38	Christina Aguilera
86	23	15	8	203	O	● Walk Like An Egyptian			3:21	Bangles
76	20	15	8	204	O	● Don't Go Breaking My Heart			4:23	Elton John & Kiki Dee
72	20	14	8	205	O	● I Can See Clearly Now			2:48	Johnny Nash
89	20	13	8	206	O	▲ Miss You Much			3:55	Janet Jackson
76	19	13	8	207	O	▲ Disco Lady			4:20	Johnnie Taylor
67	16	13	8	208	O	● The Letter			1:58	The Box Tops
85	18	12	8	209	O	▲⁴ We Are The World			6:22	USA For Africa
59	16	12	8	210	O	● Come Softly To Me			2:25	Fleetwoods
68	14	12	8	211	O	● This Guy's In Love With You			3:55	Herb Alpert

YR	WEEKS			RANK	G O L D	PEAK POSITION	PEAK WEEKS	S Y M	TIME	ARTIST
	CH	40	10							

Pos 1 4 Wks Cont'd

YR	CH	40	10	RANK	GOLD	PEAK POSITION	PEAK WEEKS	SYM	TIME	ARTIST
64	13	12	8	212 O ●		Baby Love			2:34	The Supremes
90	22	17	7	213 O ●		Vision Of Love			3:22	Mariah Carey
88	18	14	7	214 O		Roll With It			4:30	Steve Winwood
87	21	13	7	215 O		Livin' On A Prayer			4:12	Bon Jovi
75	23	16	6	216 O ●		Love Will Keep Us Together			3:15	The Captain & Tennille
58	28	13	6	217 O ●		The Chipmunk Song		[X-N]	2:17	The Chipmunks
65	11	9	6	218 O ●		Yesterday			2:04	The Beatles

Pos 1 3 Wks

YR	CH	40	10	RANK	GOLD	PEAK POSITION	PEAK WEEKS	SYM	TIME	ARTIST
60	39	33	25	219 O ●		The Twist			2:32	Chubby Checker
95	38	36	22	220 O ▲³		Gangsta's Paradise			4:00	Coolio featuring L.V.
56	26	22	18	221 O ●		The Green Door			2:11	Jim Lowe
77	33	26	17	222 O ●		How Deep Is Your Love			3:30	Bee Gees
94	30	25	16	223 O ●		Stay (I Missed You)			3:00	Lisa Loeb & Nine Stories
55	20	20	16	224 O ●		Dance With Me Henry (Wallflower)			2:15	Georgia Gibbs
56	27	22	15	225 O ●		Moonglow and Theme From "Picnic"		[I]	2:47	Morris Stoloff
80	31	21	15	226 O ▲		Another One Bites The Dust			3:32	Queen
99	32	24	14	227 O ●		Unpretty			4:38	TLC
94	22	20	14	228 O ▲		All For Love			4:39	Bryan Adams/ Rod Stewart/Sting
55	20	20	14	229 O ●		Hearts Of Stone			2:03	The Fontane Sisters
79	21	17	14	230 O ▲		Hot Stuff			3:47	Donna Summer
77	25	18	13	231 O ▲		Love Theme From "A Star Is Born" (Evergreen)			3:03	Barbra Streisand
79	27	17	13	232 O ▲		I Will Survive			3:15	Gloria Gaynor
57	26	17	13	233 O ●		You Send Me			2:41	Sam Cooke
98	36	34	12	234 O		All My Life			5:21	K-Ci & JoJo
82	28	21	12	235 O ●		Don't You Want Me			3:56	The Human League
00	24	20	12	236 O ●		Doesn't Really Matter			4:17	Janet
97	22	20	12	237 O ▲		MMMBop			3:58	Hanson
58	19	18	12	238 O ●		Witch Doctor		[N]	2:15	David Seville
81	24	17	12	239 O ●		Arthur's Theme (Best That You Can Do)			3:53	Christopher Cross
78	23	17	12	240 O ▲		Boogie Oogie Oogie			3:45	A Taste Of Honey
92	21	17	12	241 O ▲		I'm Too Sexy		[N]	2:50	Right Said Fred
00	32	27	11	242 O ●		Say My Name			4:28	Destiny's Child
80	24	19	11	243 O ▲		Woman In Love			3:48	Barbra Streisand
60	23	18	11	244 O ●		I'm Sorry			2:40	Brenda Lee
58	23	18	11	245 O ●		To Know Him, Is To Love Him			2:18	The Teddy Bears
84	23	16	11	246 O ●		Footloose			3:46	Kenny Loggins
80	21	16	11	247 O ●		Coming Up (Live At Glasgow)			3:54	Paul McCartney/Wings
70	19	16	11	248 O ●		I Think I Love You			2:50	The Partridge Family
71	18	16	11	249 O ●		Knock Three Times			2:56	Dawn
62	18	14	11	250 O ●		Peppermint Twist - Part I			2:00	Joey Dee & The Starliters
73	17	14	11	251 O ●		You're So Vain			4:25	Carly Simon
84	28	18	10	252 O ●		What's Love Got To Do With It			3:49	Tina Turner
83	25	18	10	253 O ▲		Beat It			4:11	Michael Jackson
76	25	18	10	254 O ▲		Play That Funky Music			3:12	Wild Cherry
00	20	18	10	255 O		Be With You			3:36	Enrique Iglesias
78	32	16	10	256 O ●		Baby Come Back			3:28	Player
84	24	16	10	257 O ●		Against All Odds (Take A Look At Me Now)			3:24	Phil Collins
79	21	16	10	258 O ●		Escape (The Pina Colada Song)			3:50	Rupert Holmes
59	19	16	10	259 O ●		Smoke Gets In Your Eyes			2:39	The Platters

YR	WEEKS			RANK	G O L D	PEAK POSITION PEAK WEEKS	S Y M	TIME	ARTIST
	CH	40	10						
						Pos **1** 3 Wks Cont'd			
84	26	15	10	260	O ●	I Just Called To Say I Love You		4:16	Stevie Wonder
61	17	15	10	261	O ●	Wonderland By Night . . . . [I]		3:12	Bert Kaempfert
60	27	14	10	262	O ●	Running Bear		2:33	Johnny Preston
84	21	14	10	263	O ●	Ghostbusters		4:04	Ray Parker Jr.
57	20	14	10	264	O ●	Butterfly		2:17	Andy Williams
71	18	14	10	265	O ●	Brand New Key		2:26	Melanie
66	15	13	10	266	O ●	Winchester Cathedral		2:23	New Vaudeville Band
72	14	12	10	267	O ●	A Horse With No Name		4:10	America
92	24	17	9	268	O ●	To Be With You		3:20	Mr. Big
74	23	17	9	269	O ▲	The Way We Were		3:29	Barbra Streisand
85	21	17	9	270	O ▲	Careless Whisper		4:50	Wham! Featuring George Michael
84	22	16	9	271	O ●	Karma Chameleon		4:05	Culture Club
78	20	15	9	272	O ●	MacArthur Park		3:59	Donna Summer
67	23	14	9	273	O ●	Light My Fire		2:52	The Doors
60	18	14	9	274	O ●	Save The Last Dance For Me		2:34	The Drifters
73	17	14	9	275	O ▲	Crocodile Rock		3:56	Elton John
57	17	14	9	276	O ▲	Too Much		2:30	Elvis Presley
72	18	13	9	277	O ●	Baby Don't Get Hooked On Me		3:02	Mac Davis
71	15	13	9	278	O ●	Go Away Little Girl		2:30	Donny Osmond
71	14	13	9	279	O ●	Family Affair		3:04	Sly & The Family Stone
70	14	13	9	280	O	Ain't No Mountain High Enough		3:28	Diana Ross
67	15	12	9	281	O ●	Happy Together		2:50	The Turtles
63	15	12	9	282	O ●	Hey Paula		2:25	Paul & Paula
63	14	12	9	283	O	My Boyfriend's Back		2:11	The Angels
97	20	18	8	284	O ▲	Honey		4:57	Mariah Carey
81	23	17	8	285	O ●	Kiss On My List		3:48	Daryl Hall & John Oates
90	24	16	8	286	O ▲²	Vogue		4:19	Madonna
74	21	15	8	287	O ●	Seasons In The Sun		3:24	Terry Jacks
87	21	15	8	288	O	Alone		3:38	Heart
84	24	14	8	289	O ▲	Wake Me Up Before You Go-Go		3:51	Wham!
88	21	14	8	290	O ●	Every Rose Has Its Thorn		4:20	Poison
97	20	14	8	291	O ▲	Hypnotize		3:55	The Notorious B.I.G.
85	18	14	8	292	O ●	Can't Fight This Feeling		4:54	REO Speedwagon
90	17	14	8	293	O ●	Escapade		4:41	Janet Jackson
61	16	14	8	294	O	Pony Time		2:27	Chubby Checker
72	16	14	8	295	O ●	Me And Mrs. Jones		4:42	Billy Paul
64	15	14	8	296	O ●	Oh, Pretty Woman		2:55	Roy Orbison
70	15	14	8	297	O ●	American Woman		3:51	The Guess Who
69	15	14	8	298	O ▲	Wedding Bell Blues		2:42	The 5th Dimension
85	22	13	8	299	O	Money For Nothing		4:38	Dire Straits
87	18	13	8	300	O	With Or Without You		4:56	U2
77	17	13	8	301	O	Sir Duke		3:53	Stevie Wonder
62	16	13	8	302	O	Telstar . . . . [I]		3:14	The Tornadoes
70	15	13	8	303	O	War		3:12	Edwin Starr
61	15	13	8	304	O ●	The Lion Sleeps Tonight		2:35	The Tokens
62	14	13	8	305	O ●	Soldier Boy		2:40	The Shirelles
74	17	12	8	306	O ●	The Streak . . . . [N]		3:15	Ray Stevens
63	15	12	8	307	O	Blue Velvet		2:46	Bobby Vinton
62	15	12	8	308	O ●	Hey! Baby		2:23	Bruce Channel

YR	WEEKS CH	40	10	RANK	GOLD	PEAK POSITION	PEAK WEEKS	SYM	TIME	ARTIST
						Pos **1** 3 Wks Cont'd				
63	14	12	8	309	O ●	Sukiyaki	[F]		3:05	Kyu Sakamoto
62	15	11	8	310	O ●	Duke Of Earl			2:22	Gene Chandler
65	14	11	8	311	O	Turn! Turn! Turn! (To Everything There Is A Season)			3:34	The Byrds
61	14	11	8	312	O	Blue Moon			2:15	The Marcels
63	14	11	8	313	O	I Will Follow Him			2:25	Little Peggy March
66	13	11	8	314	O ●	(You're My) Soul And Inspiration			3:00	Righteous Brothers
66	12	10	8	315	O ●	Monday, Monday			3:09	The Mamas & The Papas
67	11	10	8	316	O ●	Hello Goodbye			3:24	The Beatles
64	11	10	8	317	O	The House Of The Rising Sun			2:58	The Animals
91	20	20	7	318	O ●	Emotions			4:09	Mariah Carey
90	26	18	7	319	O ●	Love Takes Time			3:40	Mariah Carey
89	25	16	7	320	O ▲	Straight Up			4:11	Paula Abdul
72	21	16	7	321	O ●	The Candy Man			3:10	Sammy Davis, Jr.
82	23	15	7	322	O ▲	Up Where We Belong			4:00	Joe Cocker & Jennifer Warnes
86	23	15	7	323	O ●	On My Own			4:30	Patti LaBelle with Michael McDonald
90	23	14	7	324	O ●	Opposites Attract			3:45	Paula Abdul with The Wild Pair
87	21	14	7	325	O	La Bamba	[F]		2:54	Los Lobos
72	19	14	7	326	O ●	Lean On Me			3:45	Bill Withers
86	18	14	7	327	O ●	Greatest Love Of All			4:48	Whitney Houston
88	18	14	7	328	O ●	One More Try			5:50	George Michael
89	21	13	7	329	O ▲	Right Here Waiting			4:21	Richard Marx
85	19	13	7	330	O ●	Shout			3:59	Tears For Fears
86	19	13	7	331	O	Stuck With You			4:20	Huey Lewis & the News
75	17	13	7	332	O ●	Fly, Robin, Fly	[I]		3:05	Silver Convention
86	17	13	7	333	O	Rock Me Amadeus			3:10	Falco
89	19	12	7	334	O ●	Lost In Your Eyes			3:34	Debbie Gibson
89	16	12	7	335	O ●	Like A Prayer			5:19	Madonna
75	15	12	7	336	O ▲	Island Girl			3:46	Elton John
63	15	12	7	337	O	Fingertips - Pt 2			2:49	Little Stevie Wonder
68	13	12	7	338	O ●	Mrs. Robinson			4:00	Simon & Garfunkel
63	13	12	7	339	O	Walk Like A Man			2:11	The 4 Seasons
61	15	11	7	340	O ●	Take Good Care Of My Baby			2:27	Bobby Vee
90	15	11	7	341	O ▲	Step By Step			4:18	New Kids On The Block
64	13	11	7	342	O ●	Chapel Of Love			2:45	The Dixie Cups
66	12	11	7	343	O	We Can Work It Out			2:10	The Beatles
65	11	11	7	344	O ●	Mrs. Brown You've Got A Lovely Daughter			2:46	Herman's Hermits
64	11	11	7	345	O ●	I Feel Fine			2:20	The Beatles
65	14	10	7	346	O ●	I Got You Babe			3:09	Sonny & Cher
66	11	10	7	347	O ●	Summer In The City			2:39	The Lovin' Spoonful
98	32	28	6	348	O ●	Gettin' Jiggy Wit It			3:48	Will Smith
90	23	16	6	349	O	How Am I Supposed To Live Without You			4:14	Michael Bolton
76	27	15	6	350	O ●	December, 1963 (Oh, What a Night)			3:21	The Four Seasons
76	17	13	6	351	O ●	50 Ways To Leave Your Lover			3:29	Paul Simon
66	14	12	6	352	O ●	Cherish			3:00	The Association
65	13	12	6	353	O ●	Help!			2:16	The Beatles
74	15	11	6	354	O ●	(You're) Having My Baby			2:32	Paul Anka with Odia Coates
75	14	10	6	355	O ●	He Don't Love You (Like I Love You)			3:36	Tony Orlando & Dawn
75	14	12	5	356	O ●	Bad Blood			3:06	Neil Sedaka

15

YR	CH	40	10	RANK	GOLD	PEAK POSITION	PEAK WEEKS	SYM	TIME	ARTIST
						Pos 1 2 Wks				
98	52	52	26	357	O	Truly Madly Deeply			4:30	Savage Garden
55	21	21	18	358	O	Unchained Melody			2:30	Les Baxter
55	21	21	18	359	O	Learnin' The Blues			2:59	Frank Sinatra
93	24	22	16	360	O ▲	Freak Me			4:28	Silk
96	32	26	15	361	O ▲	Always Be My Baby			4:16	Mariah Carey
94	30	23	15	362	O ▲	Here Comes The Hotstepper			4:04	Ini Kamoze
93	26	22	15	363	O ▲	Weak			4:16	SWV
93	23	22	15	364	O ▲	Again			3:47	Janet Jackson
55	20	20	15	365	O ●	Ain't That A Shame			2:22	Pat Boone
98	46	34	14	366	O ●	Together Again			4:07	Janet
99	32	29	14	367	O ▲	...Baby One More Time			3:29	Britney Spears
98	23	22	14	368	O ▲	Nice & Slow			3:45	Usher
57	29	19	14	369	O ●	Round And Round			2:30	Perry Como
82	25	19	14	370	O ●	Abracadabra			3:34	The Steve Miller Band
56	24	19	14	371	O ●	The Great Pretender			2:38	The Platters
99	22	22	13	372	O	Have You Ever?			3:33	Brandy
00	26	19	13	373	O ▲	Incomplete			3:52	Sisqó
73	19	17	13	374	O	Let's Get It On			3:58	Marvin Gaye
00	55	43	12	375	O ●	Amazed			4:25	Lonestar
97	30	28	12	376	O ▲	Mo Money Mo Problems			4:09	The Notorious B.I.G. Feat. Puff Daddy & Ma$e
81	32	22	12	377	O ●	Jessie's Girl			3:14	Rick Springfield
83	25	18	12	378	O ▲	Islands In The Stream			4:08	Kenny Rogers with Dolly Parton
82	24	18	12	379	O ●	Hard To Say I'm Sorry			3:42	Chicago
78	29	22	11	380	O ●	(Love Is) Thicker Than Water			3:18	Andy Gibb
00	25	21	11	381	O ●	It's Gonna Be Me			3:10	*NSYNC
96	24	21	11	382	O ▲²	How Do U Want It			4:00	2 Pac (feat. KC & JoJo)
80	21	19	11	383	O ●	It's Still Rock And Roll To Me			2:55	Billy Joel
98	21	16	11	384	O ●	Doo Wop (That Thing)			3:58	Lauryn Hill
78	20	16	11	385	O	Three Times A Lady			3:35	Commodores
79	21	15	11	386	O	Ring My Bell			3:30	Anita Ward
69	17	15	11	387	O ▲	I Can't Get Next To You			2:53	The Temptations
68	16	15	11	388	O	Love Child			2:59	Diana Ross & The Supremes
69	16	15	11	389	O	Crimson And Clover			3:23	Tommy James & The Shondells
58	15	15	11	390	O ●	Poor Little Fool			2:29	Ricky Nelson
79	19	14	11	391	O ●	Babe			4:26	Styx
64	15	14	11	392	O	She Loves You			2:18	The Beatles
70	14	13	11	393	O ▲²	Let It Be			3:50	The Beatles
84	24	17	10	394	O ●	Hello			4:07	Lionel Richie
84	23	17	10	395	O	Owner Of A Lonely Heart			3:50	Yes
58	21	17	10	396	O ●	It's Only Make Believe			2:10	Conway Twitty
77	22	16	10	397	O ●	Torn Between Two Lovers			3:40	Mary MacGregor
59	20	16	10	398	O	Heartaches By The Number			2:39	Guy Mitchell
92	20	16	10	399	O ●	How Do You Talk To An Angel			3:40	The Heights
73	19	16	10	400	O	Keep On Truckin' (Part 1)			3:33	Eddie Kendricks
78	17	15	10	401	O ▲	You Don't Bring Me Flowers			3:14	Barbra & Neil
60	18	14	10	402	O ●	Teen Angel			2:38	Mark Dinning
60	17	14	10	403	O	My Heart Has A Mind Of Its Own			2:25	Connie Francis

YR	CH	40	10	RANK	GOLD	PEAK POSITION	SYM	TIME	ARTIST
						Pos 1 2 Wks Cont'd			
70	16	14	10	404	O	The Tears Of A Clown		2:56	Smokey Robinson & The Miracles
82	18	13	10	405	O ●	Truly		3:19	Lionel Richie
65	14	13	10	406	O	I Can't Help Myself		2:43	Four Tops
83	32	18	9	407	O ●	Baby, Come To Me		3:30	Patti Austin (with James Ingram)
81	28	18	9	408	O ●	I Love A Rainy Night		3:08	Eddie Rabbitt
81	26	18	9	409	O ●	9 To 5		2:42	Dolly Parton
75	23	18	9	410	O ●	Rhinestone Cowboy		3:08	Glen Campbell
76	26	17	9	411	O ▲	Kiss And Say Goodbye		3:29	Manhattans
91	25	17	9	412	O ▲	Gonna Make You Sweat (Everybody Dance Now)		4:03	C & C Music Factory
90	25	17	9	413	O ●	It Must Have Been Love		3:43	Roxette
81	23	17	9	414	O ●	Private Eyes		3:29	Daryl Hall & John Oates
75	21	17	9	415	O ▲	Philadelphia Freedom		5:38	The Elton John Band
76	21	17	9	416	O ●	If You Leave Me Now		3:53	Chicago
79	21	17	9	417	O ▲	Too Much Heaven		4:54	Bee Gees
84	23	16	9	418	O	Out Of Touch		3:55	Daryl Hall John Oates
83	22	16	9	419	O	Maniac		4:13	Michael Sembello
60	22	16	9	420	O	El Paso		4:40	Marty Robbins
79	25	15	9	421	O ●	Rise [I]		3:47	Herb Alpert
85	22	15	9	422	O	Broken Wings		4:29	Mr. Mister
84	20	14	9	423	O ●	Time After Time		3:59	Cyndi Lauper
84	19	14	9	424	O ▲	Let's Hear It For The Boy		4:20	Deniece Williams
84	19	14	9	425	O ●	Let's Go Crazy		3:46	Prince & the Revolution
87	18	14	9	426	O ▲	I Wanna Dance With Somebody (Who Loves Me)		4:49	Whitney Houston
71	16	14	9	427	O ●	Gypsys, Tramps & Thieves		2:36	Cher
79	20	13	9	428	O ▲	Tragedy		5:00	Bee Gees
76	18	13	9	429	O ●	Love Hangover		3:46	Diana Ross
59	18	13	9	430	O ●	Sleep Walk [I]		2:20	Santo & Johnny
61	17	13	9	431	O ●	Calcutta [I]		2:13	Lawrence Welk
65	16	13	9	432	O	You've Lost That Lovin' Feelin'		3:47	Righteous Brothers
75	16	13	9	433	O	That's The Way (I Like It)		3:06	KC & The Sunshine Band
64	15	13	9	434	O ●	I Get Around		2:12	The Beach Boys
71	15	13	9	435	O ▲	Just My Imagination (Running Away With Me)		3:39	The Temptations
65	15	13	9	436	O ●	Downtown		2:58	Petula Clark
62	15	13	9	437	O	Johnny Angel		2:16	Shelley Fabares
70	15	13	9	438	O ●	Mama Told Me (Not To Come)		2:58	Three Dog Night
68	15	13	9	439	O ●	Tighten Up		2:38	Archie Bell & The Drells
79	15	13	9	440	O ▲	No More Tears (Enough Is Enough)		4:39	Barbra Streisand & Donna Summer
64	14	13	9	441	O	Come See About Me		2:39	The Supremes
64	14	13	9	442	O	Where Did Our Love Go		2:32	The Supremes
63	17	12	9	443	O ●	Go Away Little Girl		2:07	Steve Lawrence
61	14	12	9	444	O ●	Runaround Sue		2:40	Dion
70	13	12	9	445	O	ABC		2:56	The Jackson 5
70	13	12	9	446	O	The Love You Save		2:42	The Jackson 5
71	13	12	9	447	O ●	Theme From Shaft		3:15	Isaac Hayes
64	13	12	9	448	O	Do Wah Diddy Diddy		2:19	Manfred Mann
61	17	11	9	449	O ●	Michael		2:45	The Highwaymen
65	12	11	9	450	O ●	This Diamond Ring		2:05	Gary Lewis & The Playboys
68	12	11	9	451	O ●	Hello, I Love You		2:13	The Doors

17

YR	CH	40	10	RANK	GOLD	PEAK POSITION / PEAK WEEKS	SYM	TIME	ARTIST
						Pos 1 2 Wks Cont'd			
62	37	24	8	452	O ●	Monster Mash .... [N]		3:01	Bobby "Boris" Pickett
91	25	18	8	453	O ●	The First Time		4:15	Surface
88	24	16	8	454	O ●	Look Away		3:59	Chicago
73	22	16	8	455	O ●	Bad, Bad Leroy Brown...........		3:02	Jim Croce
85	21	16	8	456	O ●	I Want To Know What Love Is........		4:58	Foreigner
98	20	16	8	457	O ●	My Heart Will Go On (Love Theme From 'Titanic')		4:36	Celine Dion
73	20	16	8	458	O ●	Top Of The World		2:56	Carpenters
73	19	16	8	459	O ●	Midnight Train To Georgia		3:55	Gladys Knight/Pips
60	18	16	8	460	O ●	Everybody's Somebody's Fool		2:40	Connie Francis
78	22	15	8	461	O ▲	Grease		3:21	Frankie Valli
87	22	15	8	462	O ●	Nothing's Gonna Stop Us Now		4:29	Starship
84	21	15	8	463	O ●	The Reflex		4:25	Duran Duran
85	19	15	8	464	O ●	The Power Of Love		3:53	Huey Lewis & The News
89	19	15	8	465	O ●	We Didn't Start The Fire........		4:29	Billy Joel
73	18	15	8	466	O ●	Brother Louie....................		3:55	Stories
61	16	15	8	467	O ●	Travelin' Man		2:12	Ricky Nelson
85	24	14	8	468	O	Everybody Wants To Rule The World..		4:10	Tears For Fears
73	22	14	8	469	O ●	Will It Go Round In Circles		3:42	Billy Preston
99	20	14	8	470	O ●	Heartbreaker		4:42	Mariah Carey (Featuring Jay-Z)
73	20	14	8	471	O ●	Half-Breed		2:42	Cher
92	20	14	8	472	O	I'll Be There		4:12	Mariah Carey
81	20	14	8	473	O ●	Rapture........................		6:33	Blondie
76	20	14	8	474	O ●	Afternoon Delight		3:12	Starland Vocal Band
91	19	14	8	475	O	I Don't Wanna Cry		4:49	Mariah Carey
57	17	14	8	476	O ●	Butterfly......................		2:21	Charlie Gracie
69	16	13	8	477	O ●	Na Na Hey Hey Kiss Him Goodbye ...		3:45	Steam
68	16	13	8	478	O ●	Judy In Disguise (With Glasses).....		2:47	John Fred & His Playboy Band
91	16	13	8	479	O ▲	Justify My Love		4:50	Madonna
64	15	13	8	480	O	My Guy.........................		2:45	Mary Wells
58	15	13	8	481	O ●	Get A Job......................		2:25	The Silhouettes
78	18	12	8	482	O	With A Little Luck		5:45	Wings
74	18	12	8	483	O ●	Kung Fu Fighting...............		3:18	Carl Douglas
75	17	12	8	484	O ●	Jive Talkin'		3:33	Bee Gees
59	16	12	8	485	O ●	Kansas City		2:21	Wilbert Harrison
71	15	12	8	486	O	Me And Bobby McGee...........		4:09	Janis Joplin
61	15	12	8	487	O ●	Quarter To Three		2:29	U.S. Bonds
69	14	12	8	488	O ●	Love Theme From Romeo & Juliet .. [I]		2:29	Henry Mancini
64	13	12	8	489	O ●	A Hard Day's Night................		2:28	The Beatles
71	12	12	8	490	O	Brown Sugar		3:50	The Rolling Stones
61	13	11	8	491	O	Hit The Road Jack		2:00	Ray Charles
66	13	11	8	492	O	You Can't Hurry Love.............		2:49	The Supremes
61	12	11	8	493	O ▲	Surrender......................		1:51	Elvis Presley
65	12	10	8	494	O ●	Stop! In The Name Of Love		2:51	The Supremes
66	11	9	8	495	O	Wild Thing		2:30	The Troggs
81	30	21	7	496	O ▲	Celebration....................		3:42	Kool & The Gang
00	24	21	7	497	O ●	What A Girl Wants		3:18	Christina Aguilera
91	21	16	7	498	O	Baby Baby		3:44	Amy Grant
91	20	16	7	499	O ●	Cream.........................		4:08	Prince & The N.P.G.
84	26	15	7	500	O ●	Caribbean Queen (No More Love On The Run)		3:39	Billy Ocean

YR	WEEKS			RANK	G O L D	PEAK POSITION	PEAK WEEKS	S Y M	TIME	ARTIST
	CH	40	10							

Pos **1** **2** Wks Cont'd

YR	CH	40	10	RANK	GOLD	PEAK POSITION	SYM	TIME	ARTIST
85	24	15	7	501	O ●	We Built This City.................		4:49	Starship
90	24	15	7	502	O ●	Black Velvet		4:45	Alannah Myles
91	23	15	7	503	O ●	All The Man That I Need............		3:43	Whitney Houston
90	22	15	7	504	O ●	Release Me........................		3:40	Wilson Phillips
61	19	15	7	505	O	Will You Love Me Tomorrow.........		2:48	The Shirelles
91	19	15	7	506	O ●	Someday		3:55	Mariah Carey
88	24	14	7	507	O ●	Never Gonna Give You Up..........		3:31	Rick Astley
88	24	14	7	508	O ●	Sweet Child O' Mine..............		5:55	Guns N' Roses
88	23	14	7	509	O ●	Anything For You..................		4:02	Gloria Estefan
85	22	14	7	510	O	St. Elmo's Fire (Man In Motion)......		4:08	John Parr
91	20	14	7	511	O ●	I Adore Mi Amor..................		4:45	Color Me Badd
73	20	14	7	512	O ●	The Night The Lights Went Out In Georgia		3:36	Vicki Lawrence
88	20	14	7	513	O	Get Outta My Dreams, Get Into My Car		4:43	Billy Ocean
91	19	14	7	514	O	Coming Out Of The Dark...........		3:55	Gloria Estefan
90	18	14	7	515	O ●	She Ain't Worth It.................		3:31	Glenn Medeiros (featuring Bobby Brown)
86	20	13	7	516	O	Kyrie............................		4:10	Mr. Mister
86	18	13	7	517	O ●	Kiss.............................		3:46	Prince & The Revolution
86	18	13	7	518	O ●	Papa Don't Preach................		3:47	Madonna
89	18	13	7	519	O	Two Hearts.......................		3:23	Phil Collins
87	17	13	7	520	O	I Still Haven't Found What I'm Looking For		4:36	U2
88	17	13	7	521	O	Man In The Mirror.................		4:55	Michael Jackson
87	17	13	7	522	O	Didn't We Almost Have It All		4:34	Whitney Houston
74	19	12	7	523	O ●	Billy, Don't Be A Hero		3:25	Bo Donaldson & The Heywoods
62	18	12	7	524	O	He's A Rebel.....................		2:25	The Crystals
87	17	12	7	525	O	I Knew You Were Waiting (For Me)....		3:57	Aretha Franklin & George Michael
73	15	12	7	526	O ●	Time In A Bottle..................		2:24	Jim Croce
66	15	12	7	527	O ●	Reach Out I'll Be There		2:58	Four Tops
63	15	12	7	528	O	I'm Leaving It Up To You		2:13	Dale & Grace
62	14	12	7	529	O	Breaking Up Is Hard To Do		2:20	Neil Sedaka
70	13	12	7	530	O ●	Thank You (Falettinme Be Mice Elf Agin)		4:47	Sly & The Family Stone
74	17	11	7	531	O ●	Annie's Song		2:58	John Denver
65	14	11	7	532	O	Help Me, Rhonda		2:45	The Beach Boys
62	13	11	7	533	O ▲	Good Luck Charm		2:23	Elvis Presley
63	13	11	7	534	O	Surf City........................		2:24	Jan & Dean
63	13	11	7	535	O	It's My Party.....................		2:19	Lesley Gore
63	13	11	7	536	O ●	Walk Right In		2:32	The Rooftop Singers
64	12	11	7	537	O ●	Rag Doll		2:31	The 4 Seasons
67	12	11	7	538	O ●	Respect		2:26	Aretha Franklin
59	14	10	7	539	O ●	A Big Hunk O' Love		2:12	Elvis Presley
63	13	10	7	540	O	Easier Said Than Done		2:08	The Essex
67	13	10	7	541	O	Kind Of A Drag...................		2:05	The Buckinghams
68	12	10	7	542	O ●	Grazing In The Grass .... [I]		2:25	Hugh Masekela
66	11	10	7	543	O	Paint It, Black...................		3:19	The Rolling Stones
73	22	17	6	544	O ●	The Most Beautiful Girl		2:42	Charlie Rich
86	23	16	6	545	O ●	How Will I Know		4:34	Whitney Houston
99	20	16	6	546	O	Bailamos		3:33	Enrique Iglesias
87	24	15	6	547	O ●	At This Moment .... [R]		4:10	Billy Vera & The Beaters
89	22	15	6	548	O ●	When I See You Smile		4:16	Bad English
81	21	15	6	549	O ●	Morning Train (Nine To Five)		3:20	Sheena Easton
88	27	14	6	550	O	The Flame		4:30	Cheap Trick

YR	WEEKS			RANK	G O L D	PEAK POSITION	PEAK WEEKS	S Y M	TIME	ARTIST
	CH	40	10							

Pos **1** **2** Wks Cont'd

YR	CH	40	10	RANK	GOLD		PEAK POSITION	SYM	TIME	ARTIST
89	23	14	6	551	O	▲	Blame It On The Rain		4:06	Milli Vanilli
89	22	14	6	552	O	●	Forever Your Girl		4:12	Paula Abdul
89	22	14	6	553	O	●	Girl I'm Gonna Miss You		4:19	Milli Vanilli
86	21	14	6	554	O		Glory Of Love.		4:20	Peter Cetera
75	21	14	6	555	O		Fame.		3:30	David Bowie
74	20	14	6	556	O	●	The Loco-Motion		2:45	Grand Funk
88	20	14	6	557	O		Could've Been		3:31	Tiffany
85	20	14	6	558	O	●	Everything She Wants		5:10	Wham!
77	20	14	6	559	O	●	Rich Girl.		2:23	Daryl Hall & John Oates
85	19	14	6	560	O		Heaven		4:03	Bryan Adams
74	18	14	6	561	O	●	TSOP (The Sound Of Philadelphia) . [I]		3:29	MFSB with The Three Degrees
58	16	14	6	562	O	▲	Hard Headed Woman		1:52	Elvis Presley
88	26	13	6	563	O	●	Don't Worry Be Happy		3:45	Bobby McFerrin
88	25	13	6	564	O	●	Groovy Kind Of Love		3:28	Phil Collins
87	24	13	6	565	O		I Think We're Alone Now		3:47	Tiffany
89	20	13	6	566	O	●	Toy Soldiers		4:52	Martika
77	20	13	6	567	O	▲	Star Wars Theme/Cantina Band . . . . [I]		3:28	Meco
86	19	13	6	568	O	●	When I Think Of You.		3:56	Janet Jackson
87	19	13	6	569	O		(I Just) Died In Your Arms		4:38	Cutting Crew
88	18	13	6	570	O		Where Do Broken Hearts Go		4:37	Whitney Houston
85	17	13	6	571	O		A View To A Kill		3:33	Duran Duran
88	17	13	6	572	O		Father Figure		5:37	George Michael
70	15	13	6	573	O	●	Everything Is Beautiful		3:29	Ray Stevens
88	20	12	6	574	O		Bad Medicine		3:52	Bon Jovi
86	20	12	6	575	O		True Colors		3:45	Cyndi Lauper
85	18	12	6	576	O	●	One More Night		4:25	Phil Collins
86	18	12	6	577	O		Amanda		4:16	Boston
74	18	12	6	578	O	●	I Can Help.		2:57	Billy Swan
87	17	12	6	579	O	●	Lean On Me		3:58	Club Nouveau
72	17	12	6	580	O	●	My Ding-A-Ling . . . . [N]		4:18	Chuck Berry
88	16	12	6	581	O		Monkey.		4:45	George Michael
73	15	11	6	582	O	●	The Morning After		2:14	Maureen McGovern
62	14	11	6	583	O	●	Sheila		2:02	Tommy Roe
63	14	11	6	584	O		If You Wanna Be Happy		2:14	Jimmy Soul
65	12	11	6	585	O		Get Off Of My Cloud		2:58	The Rolling Stones
75	14	10	6	586	O	●	Lucy In The Sky With Diamonds		5:58	Elton John
66	13	10	6	587	O	●	When A Man Loves A Woman		2:55	Percy Sledge
66	12	10	6	588	O		You Keep Me Hangin' On		2:45	The Supremes
66	12	10	6	589	O	●	Hanky Panky		2:59	Tommy James & The Shondells
70	10	10	6	590	O	▲	The Long And Winding Road		3:40	The Beatles
65	10	10	6	591	O		I Hear A Symphony		2:41	The Supremes
66	13	9	6	592	O		My Love		2:50	Petula Clark
65	11	8	6	593	O		I'm Telling You Now		2:05	Freddie & the Dreamers
66	14	12	5	594	O	◐	The Sounds Of Silence		3:05	Simon & Garfunkel
87	14	11	5	595	O		Bad.		4:05	Michael Jackson
74	24	10	5	596	O	●	I Honestly Love You		3:36	Olivia Newton-John
74	17	10	5	597	O		Rock Your Baby		3:14	George McCrae
66	10	10	5	598	O	●	Paperback Writer		2:25	The Beatles
65	10	9	5	599	O	●	Eight Days A Week.		2:43	The Beatles

Pos **1** **1** Wks

YR	CH	40	10	RANK	GOLD		PEAK POSITION	SYM	TIME	ARTIST
96	41	39	20	600	O	▲	You're Makin' Me High		4:07	Toni Braxton

YR	WEEKS			RANK	G O L D	PEAK POSITION	PEAK WEEKS	S Y M	TIME	ARTIST
	CH	40	10							

Pos **1** ¹ Wks Cont'd

YR	CH	40	10	RANK	GOLD	PEAK POSITION	SYM	TIME	ARTIST
00	41	34	19	601	O	Everything You Want		4:01	Vertical Horizon
00	40+	23+	18	602	O	With Arms Wide Open		3:52	Creed
95	36	32	17	603	O ●	Kiss From A Rose		4:43	Seal
00	32	29	15	604	O	Try Again		4:03	Aaliyah
95	21	20	15	605	O ▲	Exhale (Shoop Shoop).		3:22	Whitney Houston
58	21	17	15	606	O ●	Patricia . . . . [I]		2:28	Perez Prado
00	39	37	14	607	O ●	Bent		4:12	Matchbox Twenty
92	28	25	14	608	O ●	All 4 Love		3:30	Color Me Badd
98	27	25	14	609	O ▲	Lately		4:15	Divine
80	27	22	14	610	O ●	Do That To Me One More Time.		3:49	The Captain & Tennille
56	23	20	14	611	O ●	Hot Diggity (Dog Ziggity Boom)		2:19	Perry Como
57	28	22	13	612	O ●	Chances Are		3:00	Johnny Mathis
56	24	19	13	613	O ▲	I Want You, I Need You, I Love You		2:37	Elvis Presley
64	22	19	13	614	O	Hello, Dolly!		2:22	Louis Armstrong
57	22	19	13	615	O ●	Don't Forbid Me		2:14	Pat Boone
57	21	17	13	616	O ●	Young Love		2:29	Sonny James
79	20	15	13	617	O	Still		3:43	Commodores
57	29	18	12	618	O ●	Diana		2:29	Paul Anka
58	21	18	12	619	O ●	Tom Dooley		3:01	The Kingston Trio
98	20	18	12	620	O ▲	My All		3:48	Mariah Carey
82	21	17	12	621	O ●	I Can't Go For That (No Can Do)		3:50	Daryl Hall & John Oates
58	23	16	12	622	O ●	Catch A Falling Star.		2:25	Perry Como
58	17	14	12	623	O ●	Twilight Time		2:47	The Platters
80	26	18	11	624	O	Please Don't Go		3:43	K.C. & The Sunshine Band
59	20	17	11	625	O ●	Mr. Blue		2:18	The Fleetwoods
76	21	16	11	626	O	(Shake, Shake, Shake) Shake Your Booty.		3:06	KC & The Sunshine Band
58	19	16	11	627	O ●	Little Star		2:37	The Elegants
62	21	15	11	628	O ●	Stranger On The Shore . . . . [I]		2:52	Mr. Acker Bilk
58	18	15	11	629	O ●	Bird Dog.		2:12	The Everly Brothers
76	28	22	10	630	O ●	A Fifth Of Beethoven . . . . [I]		3:02	Walter Murphy & The Big Apple Band
97	20	19	10	631	O ▲	4 Seasons Of Loneliness.		4:51	Boyz II Men
82	27	18	10	632	O ▲	Mickey		3:36	Toni Basil
93	23	18	10	633	O ●	A Whole New World (Aladdin's Theme)		3:58	Peabo Bryson & Regina Belle
81	26	17	10	634	O ●	The Tide Is High.		3:50	Blondie
76	25	16	10	635	O ▲	Disco Duck (Part I) . . . . [N]		3:15	Rick Dees
78	22	16	10	636	O ●	If I Can't Have You		2:57	Yvonne Elliman
99	20	16	10	637	O ●	Bills, Bills, Bills		4:16	Destiny's Child
76	20	16	10	638	O ●	I Write The Songs.		3:39	Barry Manilow
57	23	15	10	639	O ●	Party Doll		2:12	Buddy Knox
69	17	15	10	640	O ●	Leaving On A Jet Plane		3:27	Peter, Paul & Mary
95	20	14	10	641	O ▲	You Are Not Alone		4:53	Michael Jackson
83	20	14	10	642	O ●	Let's Dance		4:08	David Bowie
75	17	14	10	643	O	One Of These Nights		3:28	Eagles
72	16	14	10	644	O ●	Brandy (You're A Fine Girl)		2:55	Looking Glass
76	16	14	10	645	O ●	Love Rollercoaster.		2:52	Ohio Players
70	17	13	10	646	O ●	Make It With You.		3:14	Bread
81	28	20	9	647	O ▲	Keep On Loving You		3:22	REO Speedwagon
79	24	20	9	648	O ●	Pop Muzik.		3:20	M

YR	WEEKS			RANK	GOLD	PEAK POSITION	PEAK WEEKS	SYM	TIME	ARTIST
	CH	40	10							
						Pos **1** 1 Wks Cont'd				
79	27	19	9	649 O ●		Sad Eyes			3:30	Robert John
78	31	18	9	650 O ▲		Hot Child In The City			3:06	Nick Gilder
90	25	18	9	651 O ●		Hold On			3:32	Wilson Phillips
82	27	17	9	652 O		Who Can It Be Now?			3:20	Men At Work
83	26	17	9	653 O ●		Sweet Dreams (Are Made of This)			3:36	Eurythmics
91	24	17	9	654 O ●		More Than Words			4:05	Extreme
91	23	17	9	655 O ●		I Like The Way (The Kissing Game) . . .			3:42	Hi-Five
91	25	16	9	656 O ▲		One More Try			3:24	Timmy -T-
78	24	16	9	657 O ▲		You're The One That I Want			2:49	John Travolta & Olivia Newton-John
84	24	16	9	658 O		Missing You			3:58	John Waite
91	23	16	9	659 O ●		Unbelievable			3:30	EMF
57	22	16	9	660 O ●		That'll Be The Day			2:14	The Crickets
85	21	16	9	661 O		Separate Lives			4:06	Phil Collins & Marilyn Martin
91	20	16	9	662 O		When A Man Loves A Woman			3:40	Michael Bolton
98	20	16	9	663 O		One Week			2:50	Barenaked Ladies
78	20	16	9	664 O ●		Miss You			3:31	The Rolling Stones
70	19	16	9	665 O ▲		I Want You Back			2:44	The Jackson 5
74	18	16	9	666 O ▲		Bennie And The Jets			5:20	Elton John
69	16	16	9	667 O ▲²		Come Together			4:16	The Beatles
82	28	15	9	668 O		Chariots Of Fire - Titles . . . . [I]			3:15	Vangelis
71	22	15	9	669 O ▲		Indian Reservation (The Lament Of The Cherokee Reservation Indian) . .			2:55	Raiders
77	18	15	9	670 O		Got To Give It Up (Pt. I)			4:06	Marvin Gaye
69	16	15	9	671 O ▲		Someday We'll Be Together			3:30	Diana Ross/Supremes
72	16	15	9	672 O ●		Let's Stay Together			3:15	Al Green
58	16	15	9	673 O ●		Yakety Yak			1:50	The Coasters
77	23	14	9	674 O ▲		Car Wash			3:12	Rose Royce
85	21	14	9	675 O ●		Crazy For You			3:58	Madonna
79	20	14	9	676 O ●		What A Fool Believes			3:41	The Doobie Brothers
79	19	14	9	677 O ●		Good Times			3:42	Chic
67	16	14	9	678 O ●		Incense And Peppermints			2:37	Strawberry Alarm Clock
64	15	14	9	679 O ●		Mr. Lonely			2:37	Bobby Vinton
62	17	13	9	680 O ●		The Stripper . . . . [I]			1:57	David Rose
79	15	13	9	681 O ●		Heartache Tonight			4:26	Eagles
70	14	13	9	682 O ●		Venus			3:05	The Shocking Blue
59	16	12	9	683 O ●		Why			2:30	Frankie Avalon
66	15	12	9	684 O ●		96 Tears			2:38	? & The Mysterians
66	15	12	9	685 O ●		Last Train To Clarksville			2:40	The Monkees
68	13	12	9	686 O ●		Harper Valley P.T.A.			3:12	Jeannie C. Riley
77	26	18	8	687 O ●		You Don't Have To Be A Star (To Be In My Show)			3:40	Marilyn McCoo & Billy Davis, Jr.
91	20	18	8	688 O ●		Set Adrift On Memory Bliss			3:53	PM Dawn
78	26	17	8	689 O ◒		You Needed Me			3:38	Anne Murray
88	25	17	8	690 O		Need You Tonight			3:01	INXS
77	24	17	8	691 O ●		Don't Leave Me This Way			3:35	Thelma Houston
77	21	17	8	692 O ●		You Make Me Feel Like Dancing			2:48	Leo Sayer
87	22	16	8	693 O ▲		Shake You Down			4:04	Gregory Abbott
73	21	16	8	694 O		Touch Me In The Morning			3:51	Diana Ross
92	20	16	8	695 O ●		Don't Let The Sun Go Down On Me . .			5:44	George Michael/ Elton John
74	20	16	8	696 O ●		The Joker			3:36	Steve Miller Band
85	23	15	8	697 O ●		Everytime You Go Away			4:10	Paul Young
77	22	15	8	698 O ●		Dancing Queen			3:50	Abba

YR	WEEKS			RANK	G O L D		PEAK POSITION	PEAK WEEKS		S Y M	TIME	ARTIST
	CH	40	10									

Pos 1¹ Wks Cont'd

YR	CH	40	10	RANK	GOLD		TITLE			SYM	TIME	ARTIST
86	22	15	8	699	O		The Way It Is				4:57	Bruce Hornsby & The Range
88	22	15	8	700	O		Got My Mind Set On You				3:50	George Harrison
89	21	15	8	701	O	●	Cold Hearted				3:34	Paula Abdul
75	21	15	8	702	O	●	Before The Next Teardrop Falls				2:32	Freddy Fender
77	21	15	8	703	O	●	Southern Nights				2:58	Glen Campbell
77	20	15	8	704	O	●	Blinded By The Light				3:48	Manfred Mann's Earth Band
77	19	15	8	705	O	●	Hotel California				6:08	Eagles
74	19	15	8	706	O	●	Then Came You				3:53	Dionne Warwick & the Spinners
77	17	15	8	707	O		I Wish				4:10	Stevie Wonder
75	23	14	8	708	O	●	My Eyes Adored You				3:25	Frankie Valli
85	22	14	8	709	O		Don't You (Forget About Me)				4:20	Simple Minds
72	22	14	8	710	O	●	I Am Woman				3:04	Helen Reddy
81	21	14	8	711	O	●	Medley				4:05	Stars on 45
85	21	14	8	712	O		Part-Time Lover				3:43	Stevie Wonder
90	21	14	8	713	O	▲	Blaze Of Glory				5:30	Jon Bon Jovi
92	20	14	8	714	O	●	This Used To Be My Playground				5:02	Madonna
73	20	14	8	715	O	●	Delta Dawn				3:08	Helen Reddy
90	19	14	8	716	O	●	I'm Your Baby Tonight				4:54	Whitney Houston
88	19	14	8	717	O	●	So Emotional				3:59	Whitney Houston
81	19	14	8	718	O	●	The One That You Love				4:15	Air Supply
72	15	14	8	719	O		I'll Take You There				3:19	The Staple Singers
77	20	13	8	720	O	●	Gonna Fly Now	[I]			2:45	Bill Conti
89	18	13	8	721	O	●	Don't Wanna Lose You				4:10	Gloria Estefan
75	18	13	8	722	O	●	Lovin' You				3:20	Minnie Riperton
71	16	13	8	723	O	●	Want Ads				2:34	The Honey Cone
64	15	13	8	724	O	●	Everybody Loves Somebody				2:40	Dean Martin
60	15	13	8	725	O	●	Itsy Bitsy Teenie Weenie Yellow Polkadot Bikini	[N]			2:19	Brian Hyland
72	14	13	8	726	O	●	Heart Of Gold				2:59	Neil Young
60	15	12	8	727	O	●	Alley-Oop	[N]			2:36	Hollywood Argyles
61	14	12	8	728	O		Mother-In-Law				2:25	Ernie K-Doe
71	14	12	8	729	O	●	You've Got A Friend				4:26	James Taylor
78	18	11	8	730	O	●	Too Much, Too Little, Too Late				3:00	Johnny Mathis & Deniece Williams
65	13	11	8	731	O	▲	My Girl				2:55	The Temptations
64	12	11	8	732	O		A World Without Love				2:38	Peter & Gordon
91	20	19	7	733	O		Romantic				3:48	Karyn White
90	30	17	7	734	O	●	Close To You				3:55	Maxi Priest
77	25	17	7	735	O	●	Undercover Angel				3:24	Alan O'Day
88	27	16	7	736	O	●	Wild, Wild West				3:59	The Escape Club
74	22	16	7	737	O	●	Love's Theme	[I]			3:30	Love Unlimited Orchestra
74	22	16	7	738	O	●	Show And Tell				3:28	Al Wilson
89	29	15	7	739	O	▲	Wind Beneath My Wings				4:54	Bette Midler
85	27	15	7	740	O		Take On Me				3:46	A-Ha
90	26	15	7	741	O		I Don't Have The Heart				3:52	James Ingram
89	24	15	7	742	O	●	My Prerogative				4:25	Bobby Brown
61	23	15	7	743	O	●	Please Mr. Postman				2:20	The Marvelettes

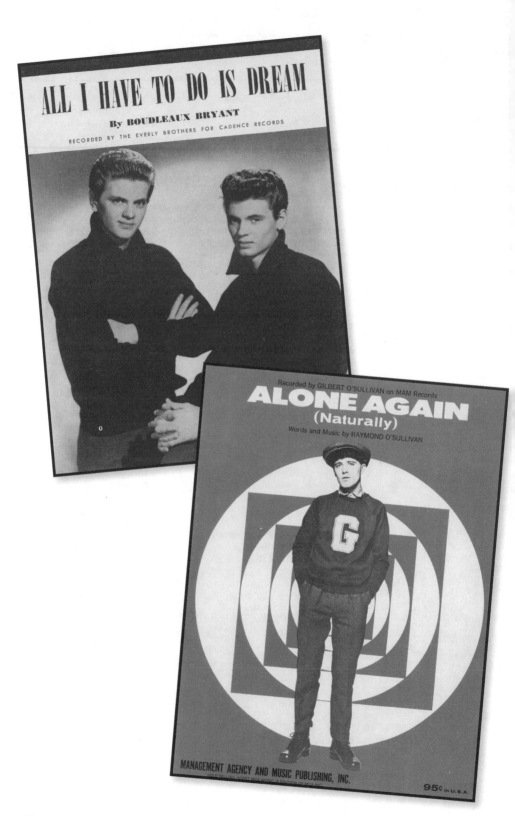

YR	WEEKS			RANK	G O L D	PEAK POSITION	PEAK WEEKS	S Y M	TIME	ARTIST
	CH	40	10							

Pos 1 ¹ Wks Cont'd

YR	CH	40	10	RANK	GOLD	PEAK POSITION / WEEKS	SYM	TIME	ARTIST
91	22	15	7	744 O ●		Love Will Never Do (Without You)		4:26	Janet Jackson
85	22	15	7	745 O ●		Saving All My Love For You		3:48	Whitney Houston
90	21	15	7	746 O ▲		Ice Ice Baby		4:53	Vanilla Ice
76	21	15	7	747 O ●		Boogie Fever		3:25	Sylvers
91	20	15	7	748 O ●		Good Vibrations		4:26	Marky Mark & The Funky Bunch
86	20	15	7	749 O		Human		3:46	Human League
75	20	15	7	750 O		Laughter In The Rain		2:50	Neil Sedaka
83	18	15	7	751 O		Tell Her About It		3:47	Billy Joel
87	28	14	7	752 O		Here I Go Again		3:52	Whitesnake
90	26	14	7	753 O ●		(Can't Live Without Your) Love And Affection		3:47	Nelson
89	23	14		754 O ●		She Drives Me Crazy		3:35	Fine Young Cannibals
86	22	14	7	755 O ●		Addicted To Love		3:59	Robert Palmer
87	22	14	7	756 O		Always		3:59	Atlantic Starr
79	21	14	7	757 O ●		Heart Of Glass		3:22	Blondie
86	21	14	7	758 O		There'll Be Sad Songs (To Make You Cry)		4:13	Billy Ocean
86	21	14	7	759 O		Sledgehammer		4:58	Peter Gabriel
86	20	14	7	760 O		West End Girls		3:55	Pet Shop Boys
77	20	14	7	761 O ●		When I Need You		4:11	Leo Sayer
87	20	14	7	762 O ●		Head To Toe		3:58	Lisa Lisa & Cult Jam
73	20	14	7	763 O ●		Frankenstein . . . . [I]		3:28	The Edgar Winter Group
74	19	14	7	764 O		You Haven't Done Nothin		3:20	Stevie Wonder
91	19	14	7	765 O		You're In Love		3:58	Wilson Phillips
87	18	14	7	766 O		Shakedown		3:59	Bob Seger
74	18	14	7	767 O ●		Nothing From Nothing		2:40	Billy Preston
75	18	14	7	768 O ●		(Hey Won't You Play) Another Somebody Done Somebody Wrong Song		3:23	B.J. Thomas
59	17	14	7	769 O		The Happy Organ . . . . [I]		2:01	Dave 'Baby' Cortez
74	17	14	7	770 O ●		Hooked On A Feeling		2:54	Blue Swede
70	15	14	7	771 O ▲		Cracklin' Rosie		2:47	Neil Diamond
72	15	14	7	772 O		Oh Girl		3:16	Chi-Lites
85	22	13	7	773 O		Miami Vice Theme . . . . [I]		2:26	Jan Hammer
86	21	13	7	774 O ●		Take My Breath Away		4:13	Berlin
80	21	13	7	775 O		Sailing		4:15	Christopher Cross
90	20	13	7	776 O		If Wishes Came True		5:09	Sweet Sensation
86	20	13	7	777 O		Sara		4:18	Starship
77	19	13	7	778 O ●		Don't Give Up On Us		3:30	David Soul
89	19	13	7	779 O ●		The Look		3:56	Roxette
77	19	13	7	780 O ●		Dreams		4:14	Fleetwood Mac
74	18	13	7	781 O ●		Sunshine On My Shoulders		3:18	John Denver
74	18	13	7	782 O ●		Band On The Run		5:09	Paul McCartney & Wings
75	18	13	7	783 O ●		Lady Marmalade		3:14	LaBelle
73	17	13	7	784 O		You Are The Sunshine Of My Life		2:52	Stevie Wonder
75	17	13	7	785 O ●		Pick Up The Pieces . . . . [I]		3:00	AWB
76	17	13	7	786 O		Theme From Mahogany (Do You Know Where You're Going To)		3:19	Diana Ross
73	16	13	7	787 O ●		Angie		4:30	The Rolling Stones
77	15	13	7	788 O ●		New Kid In Town		4:49	Eagles
77	22	12	7	789 O ●		Da Doo Ron Ron		2:46	Shaun Cassidy
76	20	12	7	790 O ●		You Should Be Dancing		4:15	Bee Gees
86	19	12	7	791 O		Venus		3:49	Bananarama
76	19	12	7	792 O		Let Your Love Flow		3:16	Bellamy Brothers
75	19	12	7	793 O ●		The Hustle . . . . [I]		3:27	Van McCoy
75	17	12	7	794 O ●		Black Water		4:17	The Doobie Brothers

YR		WEEKS		RANK	G O L D	PEAK POSITION	PEAK WEEKS	S Y M	TIME	ARTIST
	CH	40	10							
						Pos **1 1** Wks Cont'd				
62	16	12	7	795 O	●	The Loco-Motion			2:20	Little Eva
61	16	12	7	796 O		Wooden Heart			2:00	Joe Dowell
74	15	12	7	797 O	●	You're Sixteen			2:50	Ringo Starr
75	15	12	7	798 O	●	Let's Do It Again			3:28	The Staple Singers
66	15	12	7	799 O		Poor Side Of Town			3:03	Johnny Rivers
63	15	12	7	800 O		So Much In Love			2:08	The Tymes
63	15	12	7	801 O		Deep Purple			2:41	Nino Tempo & April Stevens
66	14	12	7	802 O	●	These Boots Are Made For Walkin' . . .			2:40	Nancy Sinatra
66	14	12	7	803 O	●	Good Vibrations			3:35	The Beach Boys
66	14	12	7	804 O	●	Good Lovin'			2:28	The Young Rascals
71	13	12	7	805 O	●	Uncle Albert/Admiral Halsey			4:47	Paul & Linda McCartney
68	13	12	7	806 O	●	Green Tambourine			2:22	The Lemon Pipers
74	18	11	7	807 O	●	Sundown			3:37	Gordon Lightfoot
72	16	11	7	808 O		Ben			2:42	Michael Jackson
75	16	11	7	809 O	●	Have You Never Been Mellow			3:28	Olivia Newton-John
76	16	11	7	810 O	●	Convoy	[N]		3:48	C.W. McCall
66	15	11	7	811 O	●	Strangers In The Night			2:35	Frank Sinatra
75	14	11	7	812 O	●	Listen To What The Man Said			3:53	Wings
76	14	11	7	813 O	●	Welcome Back			2:48	John Sebastian
73	14	11	7	814 O		Give Me Love - (Give Me Peace On Earth)			3:32	George Harrison
65	14	11	7	815 O		Hang On Sloopy			2:57	The McCoys
60	13	10	7	816 O		Mr. Custer	[N]		2:59	Larry Verne
66	13	10	7	817 O		Sunshine Superman			3:11	Donovan
65	13	10	7	818 O		Mr. Tambourine Man			2:18	The Byrds
64	12	10	7	819 O		Ringo	[S]		3:00	Lorne Greene
67	11	10	7	820 O		Love Is Here And Now You're Gone . .			2:35	The Supremes
65	11	10	7	821 O		Eve Of Destruction			3:28	Barry McGuire
67	12	9	7	822 O	●	Ruby Tuesday			3:12	The Rolling Stones
67	11	9	7	823 O	●	All You Need Is Love			3:57	The Beatles
76	28	19	6	824 O		Love Machine (Part 1)			2:55	The Miracles
88	40	16	6	825 O		Red Red Wine	[R]		5:21	UB40
77	23	16	6	826 O		I'm Your Boogie Man			3:58	KC & The Sunshine Band
83	21	16	6	827 O	●	Africa			4:23	Toto
88	20	16	6	828 O		Seasons Change			4:11	Exposé
88	25	15	6	829 O	●	Wishing Well			3:33	Terence Trent D'Arby
88	24	15	6	830 O	●	Baby, I Love Your Way/ Freebird Medley (Free Baby)			4:07	Will To Power
89	22	15	6	831 O	●	If You Don't Know Me By Now			3:24	Simply Red
87	21	15	6	832 O		Heaven Is A Place On Earth			4:04	Belinda Carlisle
87	21	15	6	833 O	●	(I've Had) The Time Of My Life			4:47	Bill Medley & Jennifer Warnes
86	21	15	6	834 O		The Next Time I Fall			3:43	Peter Cetera w/Amy Grant
90	20	15	6	835 O	●	Love Will Lead You Back			4:18	Taylor Dayne
86	24	14	6	836 O		You Give Love A Bad Name			3:53	Bon Jovi
83	23	14	6	837 O		Come On Eileen			4:12	Dexys Midnight Runners
86	23	14	6	838 O		Holding Back The Years			4:04	Simply Red
86	22	14	6	839 O		Higher Love			4:08	Steve Winwood
89	22	14	6	840 O		Listen To Your Heart			5:26	Roxette

Pos **1** 1 Wks Cont'd

YR	CH	40	10	RANK	GOLD	PEAK POSITION	SYM	TIME	ARTIST
89	21	14	6	841	O	● I'll Be Loving You (Forever)		3:54	New Kids On The Block
88	21	14	6	842	O	Hold On To The Nights		4:34	Richard Marx
89	21	14	6	843	O	● Baby Don't Forget My Number		4:01	Milli Vanilli
79	20	14	6	844	O	▲ Knock On Wood		3:40	Amii Stewart
89	20	14	6	845	O	The Living Years		5:30	Mike & The Mechanics
88	20	14	6	846	O	Foolish Beat		4:20	Debbie Gibson
91	19	14	6	847	O	Joyride		3:53	Roxette
91	19	14	6	848	O	● I've Been Thinking About You		3:40	Londonbeat
75	19	14	6	849	O	Best Of My Love		3:25	The Eagles
89	19	14	6	850	O	● Eternal Flame		3:56	Bangles
87	18	14	6	851	O	Open Your Heart		4:12	Madonna
99	17	14	6	852	O	● Wild Wild West		4:05	WIll Smith Feat. Dru Hill & Kool Mo Dee
85	17	14	6	853	O	● Sussudio		4:23	Phil Collins
88	23	13	6	854	O	Love Bites		5:46	Def Leppard
89	22	13	6	855	O	I'll Be There For You		5:43	Bon Jovi
85	21	13	6	856	O	Oh Sheila		3:36	Ready For The World
87	21	13	6	857	O	You Keep Me Hangin' On		4:13	Kim Wilde
86	20	13	6	858	O	These Dreams		3:46	Heart
87	20	13	6	859	O	● Lost In Emotion		3:59	Lisa Lisa & Cult Jam
74	18	13	6	860	O	● Rock Me Gently		3:28	Andy Kim
86	18	13	6	861	O	Live To Tell		4:37	Madonna
88	18	13	6	862	O	The Way You Make Me Feel		4:26	Michael Jackson
74	17	13	6	863	O	● Angie Baby		3:29	Helen Reddy
73	17	13	6	864	O	● We're An American Band		3:25	Grand Funk
89	17	13	6	865	O	Good Thing		3:22	Fine Young Cannibals
73	16	13	6	866	O	Superstition		4:06	Stevie Wonder
74	16	13	6	867	O	● Feel Like Makin' Love		2:55	Roberta Flack
60	15	13	6	868	O	I Want To Be Wanted		3:00	Brenda Lee
69	15	13	6	869	O	▲ Suspicious Minds		4:22	Elvis Presley
73	14	13	6	870	O	● Love Train		2:59	O'Jays
76	24	12	6	871	O	● Theme From S.W.A.T. . . . . [I]		2:47	Rhythm Heritage
87	22	12	6	872	O	Mony Mony "Live"		4:00	Billy Idol
79	21	12	6	873	O	▲ Don't Stop 'Til You Get Enough		5:56	Michael Jackson
74	19	12	6	874	O	● Cat's In The Cradle		3:29	Harry Chapin
88	18	12	6	875	O	Together Forever		3:20	Rick Astley
76	17	12	6	876	O	● Saturday Night		2:56	Bay City Rollers
86	17	12	6	877	O	Invisible Touch		3:26	Genesis
75	17	12	6	878	O	● Fallin' In Love		3:13	Hamilton, Joe Frank & Reynolds
89	17	12	6	879	O	▲ Hangin' Tough		3:51	New Kids On The Block
73	16	12	6	880	O	● Photograph		3:59	Ringo Starr
74	16	12	6	881	O	● Dark Lady		3:26	Cher
72	16	12	6	882	O	▲ Papa Was A Rollin' Stone		6:58	The Temptations
61	15	12	6	883	O	Moody River		2:38	Pat Boone
87	15	12	6	884	O	Jacob's Ladder		3:28	Huey Lewis & the News
72	13	12	6	885	O	● Song Sung Blue		3:15	Neil Diamond
89	18	11	6	886	O	▲ Batdance		4:06	Prince
74	17	11	6	887	O	● The Night Chicago Died		3:30	Paper Lace
87	16	11	6	888	O	Who's That Girl		3:58	Madonna
64	14	11	6	889	O	Love Me Do		2:18	The Beatles
87	14	11	6	890	O	● I Just Can't Stop Loving You		4:17	Michael Jackson
65	12	11	6	891	O	Over And Over		2:00	The Dave Clark Five
66	15	10	6	892	O	● Lightnin' Strikes		2:44	Lou Christie
90	14	10	6	893	O	Praying For Time		4:30	George Michael
63	13	10	6	894	O	Our Day Will Come		2:31	Ruby & The Romantic

YR	CH	40	10	RANK	G O L D	PEAK POSITION	PEAK WEEKS	S Y M	TIME	ARTIST

Pos 1 1 Wks Cont'd

YR	CH	40	10	RANK	GOLD	SYM	Title	TIME	ARTIST
62	13	10	6	895	O		Don't Break The Heart That Loves You	2:58	Connie Francis
67	11	10	6	896	O		The Happening	2:50	The Supremes
65	11	9	6	897	O		Ticket To Ride	3:02	The Beatles
65	10	8	6	898	O	●	I'm Henry VIII, I Am	1:49	Herman's Hermits
88	28	15	5	899	O	▲	Kokomo	3:34	The Beach Boys
75	19	15	5	900	O	●	Thank God I'm A Country Boy	2:47	John Denver
75	20	14	5	901	O	●	Shining Star	2:50	Earth, Wind & Fire
76	18	14	5	902	O		Rock'n Me	3:05	Steve Miller
60	18	14	5	903	O		Stay	1:50	Maurice Williams & Zodiacs
89	28	13	5	904	O	●	When I'm With You	3:54	Sheriff
89	21	13	5	905	O	●	Rock On	3:21	Michael Damian
77	19	13	5	906	O	●	Looks Like We Made It	3:29	Barry Manilow
79	19	13	5	907	O	●	Love You Inside Out	3:48	Bee Gees
90	18	13	5	908	O	●	I'll Be Your Everything	3:58	Tommy Page
91	16	13	5	909	O		The Promise Of A New Day	4:09	Paula Abdul
89	15	13	5	910	O		Satisfied	4:10	Richard Marx
74	17	12	5	911	O	●	You Ain't Seen Nothing Yet	3:29	Bachman-Turner Overdrive
75	17	12	5	912	O	●	Please Mr. Postman	2:48	Carpenters
75	16	12	5	913	O	●	Mandy	3:20	Barry Manilow
90	16	12	5	914	O	●	Black Cat	4:25	Janet Jackson
88	14	11	5	915	O		Dirty Diana	4:37	Michael Jackson
74	18	10	5	916	O	●	Rock The Boat	3:03	The Hues Corporation
75	16	10	5	917	O		You're No Good	3:40	Linda Ronstadt
74	14	10	5	918	O	●	I Shot The Sheriff	3:30	Eric Clapton
60	13	10	5	919	O		Georgia On My Mind	3:37	Ray Charles
64	12	10	5	920	O		Leader Of The Pack	2:48	The Shangri-Las
65	11	10	5	921	O		Game Of Love	2:04	Wayne Fontana & The Mindbenders
65	11	10	5	922	O		Back In My Arms Again	2:50	The Supremes
72	11	9	5	923	O	●	Black & White	3:24	Three Dog Night
67	10	9	5	924	O	●	Penny Lane	3:00	The Beatles
61	17	15	4	925	O		Running Scared	2:10	Roy Orbison
75	18	13	4	926	O	●	I'm Sorry	3:29	John Denver
75	17	12	4	927	O	●	Fire	3:12	Ohio Players
75	16	12	4	928	O		Sister Golden Hair	3:16	America
00	20	11	4	929	O	●	Thank God I Found You	4:14	Mariah With Joe & 98°
75	15	9	4	930	O		Get Down Tonight	3:21	K.C. & The Sunshine Band
74	12	9	4	931	O	●	Can't Get Enough Of Your Love, Babe	3:24	Barry White
74	15	11	3	932	O		Whatever Gets You Thru The Night	3:16	John Lennon/Plastic Ono Nuclear Band

Pos 2 10 Wks

YR	CH	40	10	RANK	GOLD	SYM	Title	TIME	ARTIST
81	23	19	15	933	O	●	Waiting For A Girl Like You	4:35	Foreigner

Pos 2 9 Wks

YR	CH	40	10	RANK	GOLD	SYM	Title	TIME	ARTIST
98	42	41	23	934	O	▲	You're Still The One	3:31	Shania Twain
96	41	35	16	935	O	●	I Love You Always Forever	3:56	Donna Lewis

YR	CH	40	10	RANK	GOLD	PEAK POSITION / PEAK WEEKS	SYM	TIME	ARTIST
						Pos 2 — 8 Wks			
98	29	27	20	936	○	▲ Nobody's Supposed To Be Here		4:19	Deborah Cox
99	37	33	15	937	○	Back At One		6:45	Brian McKnight
92	27	24	15	938	○	▲ If I Ever Fall In Love		3:05	Shai
57	26	21	14	939	○	● Little Darlin'		2:05	The Diamonds
						Pos 2 — 7 Wks			
93	45	41	24	940	○	▲^{4} Whoomp! (There It Is)		4:27	Tag Team
97	47	40	23	941	○	▲ You Make Me Wanna...		3:38	Usher
55	20	20	16	942	○	● The Crazy Otto	[I]	2:58	Johnny Maddox
						Pos 2 — 6 Wks			
55	25	25	19	943	○	● Moments To Remember		3:14	The Four Lads
94	33	27	14	944	○	● All I Wanna Do		4:06	Sheryl Crow
92	33	24	14	945	○	▲ Baby-Baby-Baby		4:05	TLC
92	24	20	11	946	○	● Sometimes Love Just Ain't Enough		4:26	Patty Smyth with Don Henley
82	18	14	10	947	○	Open Arms		3:21	Journey
78	20	15	9	948	○	● Baker Street		4:08	Gerry Rafferty
63	18	13	9	949	○	Louie Louie		2:24	The Kingsmen
						Pos 2 — 5 Wks			
00	53	42	19	950	○	● Breathe		4:04	Faith Hill
96	30	29	19	951	○	▲ It's All Coming Back To Me Now		5:28	Celine Dion
82	23	18	11	952	○	● Rosanna		3:59	Toto
62	16	14	10	953	○	▲ Return To Sender		2:05	Elvis Presley
80	23	15	9	954	○	▲ More Than I Can Say		3:40	Leo Sayer
83	22	15	8	955	○	▲ Electric Avenue		3:47	Eddy Grant
						Pos 2 — 4 Wks			
97	69	61	32	956	○	▲^{3} How Do I Live		4:18	LeAnn Rimes
57	38	26	18	957	○	● So Rare		2:30	Jimmy Dorsey
97	35	33	17	958	○	▲ Don't Let Go (Love)		4:04	En Vogue
96	34	31	16	959	○	▲ I Believe I Can Fly		4:42	R. Kelly
82	28	22	16	960	○	● Hurts So Good		3:35	John Cougar
57	27	22	15	961	○	● Bye Bye Love		2:17	The Everly Brothers
56	24	19	14	962	○	● No, Not Much!		3:12	The Four Lads
92	26	23	12	963	○	▲ Tears In Heaven		4:29	Eric Clapton
95	25	21	12	964	○	● Candy Rain		4:28	Soul For Real
97	30	25	11	965	○	● Bitch		4:08	Meredith Brooks
91	22	19	11	966	○	● It's So Hard To Say Goodbye To Yesterday		2:45	Boyz II Men
56	21	17	11	967	○	Blue Suede Shoes		2:14	Carl Perkins
82	21	16	11	968	○	Don't Talk To Strangers		3:00	Rick Springfield
94	26	24	10	969	○	● I'll Remember		4:13	Madonna
80	27	17	10	970	○	● All Out Of Love		3:51	Air Supply
91	23	16	10	971	○	▲^{2} I Wanna Sex You Up		4:09	Color Me Badd
60	20	15	10	972	○	● Last Date	[I]	2:20	Floyd Cramer
83	18	15	10	973	○	Say It Isn't So		3:56	Daryl Hall-John Oates
80	21	17	9	974	○	Ride Like The Wind		3:54	Christopher Cross
84	21	15	9	975	○	▲ Dancing In The Dark		3:59	Bruce Springsteen
60	20	15	9	976	○	Greenfields		3:00	The Brothers Four
70	17	14	9	977	○	● We've Only Just Begun		3:09	Carpenters
58	21	13	9	978	○	● Great Balls Of Fire		1:50	Jerry Lee Lewis
83	21	19	8	979	○	Shame On The Moon		4:55	Bob Seger & Silver Bullet Band
84	18	14	8	980	○	● The Wild Boys		4:14	Duran Duran

YR	CH	40	10	RANK	GOLD	PEAK POSITION	SYM	TIME	ARTIST
						Pos **2** 4 Wks Cont'd			
66	12	11	8	981	O ●	Snoopy Vs. The Red Baron . . . . [N]		2:43	The Royal Guardsmen
64	26	16	7	982	O	Twist And Shout		2:33	The Beatles
63	15	12	7	983	O	Can't Get Used To Losing You		2:19	Andy Williams
68	13	11	7	984	O ●	(Theme From) Valley Of The Dolls		3:35	Dionne Warwick
87	19	14	6	985	O	Looking For A New Love		3:58	Jody Watley
73	14	11	6	986	O ●	Dueling Banjos . . . . [I]		3:17	Eric Weissberg & Steve Mandell
75	10	7	5	987	O	Calypso		3:32	John Denver
						Pos **2** 3 Wks			
93	36	30	18	988	O ▲	All That She Wants		3:27	Ace Of Base
98	24	24	16	989	O ▲	My Way		3:33	Usher
56	39	22	16	990	O ●	Honky Tonk (Parts 1 & 2) . . . . [I]		5:35	Bill Doggett
57	27	21	16	991	O ●	Blueberry Hill		2:14	Fats Domino
92	28	23	15	992	O ▲²	Rump Shaker		3:51	Wreckx-N-Effect
56	27	22	15	993	O ●	Whatever Will Be, Will Be (Que Sera, Sera)		2:01	Doris Day
99	28	21	15	994	O ▲	Heartbreak Hotel		3:59	Whitney Houston (Feat. Faith Evans & Kelly Price)
95	29	27	14	995	O ▲	Don't Take It Personal (just one of dem days)		4:12	Monica
55	18	17	14	996	O ●	I Hear You Knocking		2:20	Gale Storm
92	30	22	13	997	O ●	My Lovin' (You're Never Gonna Get It) .		4:32	En Vogue
00	26+	21+	13	998	O	Case Of The Ex (Whatcha Gonna Do) .		3:50	Mya
79	26	20	12	999	O ▲	Y.M.C.A.		3:42	Village People
60	23	20	12	1000	O ●	He'll Have To Go		2:16	Jim Reeves

THE YEARS

This section lists each year's 40 biggest hits. These rankings are based on the Top 1000 ranking system.

You will find hundreds of additional hits in these yearly Top 40 rankings that do not appear in the Top 1000 ranking. A break separates Top 1000-ranked titles from those that do not rank within the Top 1000.

Columnar headings show the following data:

RANK: Top 1000 ranking
PK DATE: Date song reached its peak position
PK WKS: Total weeks song held its peak position
PK POS: Highest charted position song attained

1955   Top 40 Hits

RANK	PK DATE	PK WKS	PK POS	TITLE	ARTIST
14	4/30	10	1	1. Cherry Pink And Apple Blossom White	Perez Prado
16	2/12	10	1	2. Sincerely	The McGuire Sisters
26	7/09	8	1	3. (We're Gonna) Rock Around The Clock	Bill Haley & His Comets
29	11/26	8	1	4. Sixteen Tons	"Tennessee" Ernie Ford
60	10/08	6	1	5. Love Is A Many-Splendored Thing	Four Aces
64	9/03	6	1	6. The Yellow Rose Of Texas	Mitch Miller
91	3/26	5	1	7. The Ballad Of Davy Crockett	Bill Hayes
134	10/29	4	1	8. Autumn Leaves	Roger Williams
160	1/01	4	1	9. Let Me Go Lover	Joan Weber
224	5/14	3	1	10. Dance With Me Henry (Wallflower)	Georgia Gibbs
229	2/05	3	1	11. Hearts Of Stone	The Fontane Sisters
358	5/14	2	1	12. Unchained Melody	Les Baxter
359	7/09	2	1	13. Learnin' The Blues	Frank Sinatra
365	9/17	2	1	14. Ain't That A Shame	Pat Boone
942	3/12	7	2	15. The Crazy Otto	Johnny Maddox
943	10/29	6	2	16. Moments To Remember	The Four Lads
996	12/10	3	2	17. I Hear You Knocking	Gale Storm
	3/05	3	2	18. Ko Ko Mo (I Love You So)	Perry Como
	3/05	1	2	19. Melody Of Love	Billy Vaughn
	7/09	1	2	20. A Blossom Fell	Nat "King" Cole
	4/02	1	2	21. Tweedle Dee	Georgia Gibbs
	4/09	1	2	22. How Important Can It Be?	Joni James
	1/01	4	3	23. The Naughty Lady Of Shady Lane	The Ames Brothers
	11/26	2	3	24. The Shifting, Whispering Sands	Rusty Draper
	6/04	1	3	25. Unchained Melody	Al Hibbler
	3/12	1	3	26. Melody Of Love	Four Aces
	9/17	1	3	27. The Yellow Rose Of Texas	Johnny Desmond
	10/08	1	3	28. Seventeen	The Fontane Sisters
	2/26	1	3	29. That's All I Want From You	Jaye P. Morgan
	3/12	1	3	30. Earth Angel	The Crew-Cuts
	8/13	1	4	31. Hard To Get	Gisele MacKenzie
	12/31	1	4	32. He	Al Hibbler
	5/14	4	5	33. Ballad Of Davy Crockett	"Tennessee" Ernie Ford
	10/22	4	5	34. The Shifting Whispering Sands (Parts 1 & 2)	Billy Vaughn
	11/05	3	5	35. Only You (And You Alone)	The Platters
	11/26	3	5	36. Love And Marriage	Frank Sinatra
	5/21	1	5	37. Ballad Of Davy Crockett	Fess Parker
	10/15	1	5	38. Tina Marie	Perry Como
	7/23	1	5	39. Something's Gotta Give	The McGuire Sisters
	9/10	1	5	40. Maybellene	Chuck Berry

Top 40 Hits   1956

RANK	PK DATE	PK WKS	PK POS	TITLE	ARTIST
10	8/18	11	1	1. Don't Be Cruel /	Elvis Presley
				Hound Dog	Elvis Presley
17	12/08	10	1	2. Singing The Blues	Guy Mitchell
28	6/16	8	1	3. The Wayward Wind	Gogi Grant
30	4/21	8	1	4. Heartbreak Hotel	Elvis Presley
62	2/18	6	1	5. Rock And Roll Waltz	Kay Starr
63	3/17	6	1	6. The Poor People Of Paris	Les Baxter
66	1/07	6	1	7. Memories Are Made Of This	Dean Martin
94	11/03	5	1	8. Love Me Tender	Elvis Presley
96	8/04	5	1	9. My Prayer	The Platters
137	2/25	4	1	10. Lisbon Antigua	Nelson Riddle
144	7/28	4	1	11. I Almost Lost My Mind	Pat Boone
221	11/03	3	1	12. The Green Door	Jim Lowe
225	6/02	3	1	13. Moonglow and Theme From "Picnic"	Morris Stoloff
371	2/18	2	1	14. The Great Pretender	The Platters
611	5/05	1	1	15. Hot Diggity (Dog Ziggity Boom)	Perry Como
613	7/28	1	1	16. I Want You, I Need You, I Love You	Elvis Presley
962	3/17	4	2	17. No, Not Much!	The Four Lads
967	5/19	4	2	18. Blue Suede Shoes	Carl Perkins
990	10/06	3	2	19. Honky Tonk (Parts 1 & 2)	Bill Doggett
993	8/18	3	2	20. Whatever Will Be, Will Be (Que Sera, Sera)	Doris Day
	10/13	2	2	21. Canadian Sunset	Hugo Winterhalter with Eddie Heywood
	8/18	2	2	22. Allegheny Moon	Patti Page
	10/27	1	2	23. Just Walking In The Rain	Johnnie Ray
	6/16	1	2	24. Ivory Tower	Cathy Carr
	6/16	3	3	25. Standing On The Corner	The Four Lads
	7/14	2	3	26. I'm In Love Again	Fats Domino
	11/10	1	3	27. True Love	Bing Crosby & Grace Kelly
	8/25	1	3	28. The Flying Saucer (Parts 1 & 2)	Buchanan & Goodman
	7/07	4	4	29. On The Street Where You Live	Vic Damone
	5/19	3	4	30. (You've Got) The Magic Touch	The Platters
	1/07	1	4	31. Band Of Gold	Don Cherry
	4/07	1	4	32. I'll Be Home	Pat Boone
	10/06	1	4	33. Tonight You Belong To Me	Patience & Prudence
	6/02	1	4	34. Moonglow And Theme From "Picnic"	George Cates
	7/21	1	4	35. More	Perry Como
	5/12	2	5	36. A Tear Fell	Teresa Brewer
	7/14	2	5	37. Born To Be With You	The Chordettes
	10/20	1	5	38. Friendly Persuasion (Thee I Love)	Pat Boone
	1/14	1	5	39. Memories Are Made Of This	Gale Storm
	2/11	4	6	40. See You Later, Alligator	Bill Haley & His Comets

1957   Top 40 Hits

RANK	PK DATE	PK WKS	PK POS	TITLE	ARTIST
21	4/13	9	1	1. All Shook Up	Elvis Presley
39	6/03	7	1	2. Love Letters In The Sand	Pat Boone
42	10/21	7	1	3. Jailhouse Rock	Elvis Presley
44	7/08	7	1	4. (Let Me Be Your) Teddy Bear	Elvis Presley
69	12/16	6	1	5. April Love	Pat Boone
73	2/16	6	1	6. Young Love	Tab Hunter
89	8/19	5	1	7. Tammy	Debbie Reynolds
146	9/23	4	1	8. Honeycomb	Jimmie Rodgers
153	10/14	4	1	9. Wake Up Little Susie	The Everly Brothers
233	12/02	3	1	10. You Send Me	Sam Cooke
264	3/30	3	1	11. Butterfly	Andy Williams
276	2/09	3	1	12. Too Much	Elvis Presley
369	4/06	2	1	13. Round And Round	Perry Como
476	4/13	2	1	14. Butterfly	Charlie Gracie
612	10/21	1	1	15. Chances Are	Johnny Mathis
615	2/09	1	1	16. Don't Forbid Me	Pat Boone
616	2/09	1	1	17. Young Love	Sonny James
618	9/09	1	1	18. Diana	Paul Anka
639	3/30	1	1	19. Party Doll	Buddy Knox
660	9/23	1	1	20. That'll Be The Day	The Crickets
939	4/06	8	2	21. Little Darlin'	The Diamonds
957	6/17	4	2	22. So Rare	Jimmy Dorsey
961	6/17	4	2	23. Bye Bye Love	The Everly Brothers
991	1/19	3	2	24. Blueberry Hill	Fats Domino
	1/05	2	2	25. Love Me	Elvis Presley
	3/16	2	2	26. Teen-Age Crush	Tommy Sands
	6/03	1	2	27. A White Sport Coat (And A Pink Carnation)	Marty Robbins
	12/16	1	2	28. Raunchy	Bill Justis
	6/10	1	2	29. A Teenager's Romance	Ricky Nelson
	8/05	4	3	30. I'm Gonna Sit Right Down And Write Myself A Letter	Billy Williams
	12/16	1	3	31. Kisses Sweeter Than Wine	Jimmie Rodgers
	12/30	3	3	32. Peggy Sue	Buddy Holly
	5/13	3	3	33. School Day	Chuck Berry
	9/09	2	3	34. Whole Lot Of Shakin' Going On	Jerry Lee Lewis
	11/04	2	3	35. Silhouettes	The Rays
	7/29	1	3	36. Searchin'	The Coasters
	7/29	1	3	37. Old Cape Cod	Patti Page
	1/19	1	3	38. Moonlight Gambler	Frankie Laine
	1/12	1	3	39. Hey! Jealous Lover	Frank Sinatra
	4/06	1	3	40. Marianne	The Hilltoppers

Top 40 Hits   1958

RANK	PK DATE	PK WKS	PK POS	TITLE	ARTIST
47	1/06	7	1	1. At The Hop	Danny & The Juniors
76	9/29	6	1	2. It's All In The Game	Tommy Edwards
84	6/09	6	1	3. The Purple People Eater	Sheb Wooley
103	5/12	5	1	4. All I Have To Do Is Dream	The Everly Brothers
106	3/17	5	1	5. Tequila	The Champs
111	2/10	5	1	6. Don't	Elvis Presley
118	8/18	5	1	7. Nel Blu Dipinto Di Blu (Volare)	Domenico Modugno
155	2/17	4	1	8. Sugartime	The McGuire Sisters
191	4/14	4	1	9. He's Got The Whole World (In His Hands)	Laurie London
217	12/22	4	1	10. The Chipmunk Song	The Chipmunks
238	4/28	3	1	11. Witch Doctor	David Seville
245	12/01	3	1	12. To Know Him, Is To Love Him	The Teddy Bears
390	8/04	2	1	13. Poor Little Fool	Ricky Nelson
396	11/10	2	1	14. It's Only Make Believe	Conway Twitty
481	2/24	2	1	15. Get A Job	The Silhouettes
562	7/21	2	1	16. Hard Headed Woman	Elvis Presley
606	7/28	1	1	17. Patricia	Perez Prado
619	11/17	1	1	18. Tom Dooley	The Kingston Trio
622	3/24	1	1	19. Catch A Falling Star	Perry Como
623	4/21	1	1	20. Twilight Time	The Platters
627	8/25	1	1	21. Little Star	The Elegants
629	8/25	1	1	22. Bird Dog	The Everly Brothers
673	7/21	1	1	23. Yakety Yak	The Coasters
978	1/06	4	2	24. Great Balls Of Fire	Jerry Lee Lewis
	3/10	3	2	25. 26 Miles (Santa Catalina)	The Four Preps
	1/13	3	2	26. Stood Up	Ricky Nelson
	3/17	3	2	27. Sweet Little Sixteen	Chuck Berry
	10/13	2	2	28. Rock-in Robin	Bobby Day
	3/31	2	2	29. Lollipop	The Chordettes
	1/06	1	2	30. All The Way	Frank Sinatra
	4/28	1	2	31. Wear My Ring Around Your Neck	Elvis Presley
	12/15	1	2	32. Problems	The Everly Brothers
	6/16	3	3	33. Secretly	Jimmie Rodgers
	10/20	3	3	34. Topsy II	Cozy Cole
	6/09	2	3	35. Big Man	The Four Preps
	2/10	2	3	36. Short Shorts	Royal Teens
	8/18	1	3	37. My True Love	Jack Scott
	8/04	1	3	38. Splish Splash	Bobby Darin
	3/24	1	3	39. Are You Sincere	Andy Williams
	3/10	5	4	40. A Wonderful Time Up There	Pat Boone

PK RANK	PK DATE	PK WKS	POS	TITLE	ARTIST
20	10/05	9	1	1. Mack The Knife	Bobby Darin
72	6/01	6	1	2. The Battle Of New Orleans	Johnny Horton
116	3/09	5	1	3. Venus	Frankie Avalon
173	2/09	4	1	4. Stagger Lee	Lloyd Price
176	8/24	4	1	5. The Three Bells	The Browns
177	7/13	4	1	6. Lonely Boy	Paul Anka
210	4/13	4	1	7. Come Softly To Me	Fleetwoods
259	1/19	3	1	8. Smoke Gets In Your Eyes	The Platters
398	12/14	2	1	9. Heartaches By The Number	Guy Mitchell
430	9/21	2	1	10. Sleep Walk	Santo & Johnny
485	5/18	2	1	11. Kansas City	Wilbert Harrison
539	8/10	2	1	12. A Big Hunk O' Love	Elvis Presley
625	11/16	1	1	13. Mr. Blue	The Fleetwoods
683	12/28	1	1	14. Why	Frankie Avalon
769	5/11	1	1	15. The Happy Organ	Dave 'Baby' Cortez
	10/05	3	2	16. Put Your Head On My Shoulder	Paul Anka
	6/15	3	2	17. Personality	Lloyd Price
	3/09	3	2	18. Charlie Brown	The Coasters
	2/23	2	2	19. Donna	Ritchie Valens
	2/09	2	2	20. 16 Candles	The Crests
	1/19	2	2	21. My Happiness	Connie Francis
	5/11	2	2	22. Sorry (I Ran All the Way Home)	The Impalas
	8/24	2	2	23. Sea Of Love	Phil Phillips
	6/08	1	2	24. Dream Lover	Bobby Darin
	11/30	1	2	25. Don't You Know	Della Reese
	8/17	1	2	26. There Goes My Baby	The Drifters
	2/02	1	2	27. The All American Boy	Bill Parsons
	4/27	1	2	28. (Now and Then There's) A Fool Such As I	Elvis Presley
	8/03	3	3	29. My Heart Is An Open Book	Carl Dobkins, Jr.
	4/13	2	3	30. Pink Shoe Laces	Dodie Stevens
	12/28	2	3	31. The Big Hurt	Miss Toni Fisher
	9/14	2	3	32. I'm Gonna Get Married	Lloyd Price
	7/20	2	3	33. Tiger	Fabian
	3/16	2	3	34. Alvin's Harmonica	The Chipmunks
	4/06	1	3	35. It's Just A Matter Of Time	Brook Benton
	8/24	1	3	36. Lavender-Blue	Sammy Turner
	9/21	3	4	37. ('Til) I Kissed You	The Everly Brothers
	7/13	3	4	38. Waterloo	Stonewall Jackson
	10/19	2	4	39. Teen Beat	Sandy Nelson
	6/01	2	4	40. Quiet Village	Martin Denny

RANK	PK DATE	PK WKS	PK POS	TITLE	ARTIST
25	2/22	9	1	1. The Theme From "A Summer Place"	Percy Faith
82	11/28	6	1	2. Are You Lonesome To-night?	Elvis Presley
105	8/15	5	1	3. It's Now Or Never	Elvis Presley
124	5/23	5	1	4. Cathy's Clown	The Everly Brothers
179	4/25	4	1	5. Stuck On You	Elvis Presley
244	7/18	3	1	6. I'm Sorry	Brenda Lee
262	1/18	3	1	7. Running Bear	Johnny Preston
274	10/17	3	1	8. Save The Last Dance For Me	The Drifters
402	2/08	2	1	9. Teen Angel	Mark Dinning
403	9/26	2	1	10. My Heart Has A Mind Of Its Own	Connie Francis
420	1/04	2	1	11. El Paso	Marty Robbins
460	6/27	2	1	12. Everybody's Somebody's Fool	Connie Francis
219	9/19	1	1	13. The Twist	Chubby Checker
				re-entered at #1 in 1962	
725	8/08	1	1	14. Itsy Bitsy Teenie Weenie Yellow Polkadot Bikini	Brian Hyland
727	7/11	1	1	15. Alley-Oop	Hollywood Argyles
816	10/10	1	1	16. Mr. Custer	Larry Verne
868	10/24	1	1	17. I Want To Be Wanted	Brenda Lee
903	11/21	1	1	18. Stay	Maurice Williams & Zodiacs
919	11/14	1	1	19. Georgia On My Mind	Ray Charles
972	11/28	4	2	20. Last Date	Floyd Cramer
976	4/18	4	2	21. Greenfields	The Brothers Four
1000	3/07	3	2	22. He'll Have To Go	Jim Reeves
	10/03	2	2	23. Chain Gang	Sam Cooke
	4/04	2	2	24. Puppy Love	Paul Anka
	2/29	1	2	25. Handy Man	Jimmy Jones
	8/29	1	2	26. Walk—Don't Run	The Ventures
	7/25	1	2	27. Only The Lonely (Know How I Feel)	Roy Orbison
	3/28	1	2	28. Wild One	Bobby Rydell
	11/14	1	2	29. Poetry In Motion	Johnny Tillotson
	5/23	3	3	30. Good Timin'	Jimmy Jones
	6/13	2	3	31. Burning Bridges	Jack Scott
	12/12	1	3	32. A Thousand Stars	Kathy Young
	5/02	1	3	33. Sixteen Reasons	Connie Stevens
	4/25	1	3	34. Sink The Bismarck	Johnny Horton
	1/11	1	3	35. Way Down Yonder In New Orleans	Freddie Cannon
	2/08	1	3	36. Where Or When	Dion & The Belmonts
	11/14	1	3	37. You Talk Too Much	Joe Jones
	5/09	2	4	38. Night	Jackie Wilson
	5/30	2	4	39. He'll Have To Stay	Jeanne Black
	7/04	2	4	40. Because They're Young	Duane Eddy

1961   Top 40 Hits

RANK	PK DATE	PK WKS	PK POS	TITLE	ARTIST
48	7/10	7	1	1. Tossin' And Turnin'	Bobby Lewis
119	11/06	5	1	2. Big Bad John	Jimmy Dean
195	4/24	4	1	3. Runaway	Del Shannon
261	1/09	3	1	4. Wonderland By Night	Bert Kaempfert
294	2/27	3	1	5. Pony Time	Chubby Checker
304	12/18	3	1	6. The Lion Sleeps Tonight	The Tokens
312	4/03	3	1	7. Blue Moon	The Marcels
340	9/18	3	1	8. Take Good Care Of My Baby	Bobby Vee
431	2/13	2	1	9. Calcutta	Lawrence Welk
444	10/23	2	1	10. Runaround Sue	Dion
449	9/04	2	1	11. Michael	The Highwaymen
467	5/29	2	1	12. Travelin' Man	Ricky Nelson
487	6/26	2	1	13. Quarter To Three	U.S. Bonds
491	10/09	2	1	14. Hit The Road Jack	Ray Charles
493	3/20	2	1	15. Surrender	Elvis Presley
505	1/30	2	1	16. Will You Love Me Tomorrow	The Shirelles
728	5/22	1	1	17. Mother-In-Law	Ernie K-Doe
743	12/11	1	1	18. Please Mr. Postman	The Marvelettes
796	8/28	1	1	19. Wooden Heart	Joe Dowell
883	6/19	1	1	20. Moody River	Pat Boone
925	6/05	1	1	21. Running Scared	Roy Orbison
	7/10	3	2	22. The Boll Weevil Song	Brook Benton
	7/31	3	2	23. I Like It Like That, Part 1	Chris Kenner
	10/23	2	2	24. Bristol Stomp	The Dovells
	4/03	2	2	25. Apache	Jorgen Ingmannr
	9/25	2	2	26. The Mountain's High	Dick & DeeDee
	1/23	1	2	27. Exodus	Ferrante & Teicher
	6/26	1	2	28. Raindrops	Dee Clark
	2/20	1	2	29. Shop Around	The Miracles
	12/25	1	2	30. Run To Him	Bobby Vee
	10/09	1	2	31. Crying	Roy Orbison
	5/29	1	2	32. Daddy's Home	Shep & The Limelites
	3/27	2	3	33. Dedicated To The One I Love	The Shirelles
	5/08	2	3	34. A Hundred Pounds Of Clay	Gene McDaniels
	12/04	2	3	35. Goodbye Cruel World	James Darren
	3/06	2	3	36. Wheels	The String-A-Longs
	8/07	2	3	37. Last Night	Mar-Keys
	11/13	2	3	38. Fool #1	Brenda Lee
	9/11	2	3	39. My True Story	The Jive Five
	3/20	1	3	40. Don't Worry	Marty Robbins

Top 40 Hits   1962

RANK	PK DATE	PK WKS	PK POS	TITLE	ARTIST
110	6/02	5	1	1. I Can't Stop Loving You	Ray Charles
117	11/17	5	1	2. Big Girls Don't Cry	The 4 Seasons
130	9/15	5	1	3. Sherry	The 4 Seasons
180	7/14	4	1	4. Roses Are Red (My Love)	Bobby Vinton
250	1/27	3	1	5. Peppermint Twist - Part I	Joey Dee & the Starliters
302	12/22	3	1	6. Telstar	The Tornadoes
305	5/05	3	1	7. Soldier Boy	The Shirelles
308	3/10	3	1	8. Hey! Baby	Bruce Channel
310	2/17	3	1	9. Duke Of Earl	Gene Chandler
219	1/13	2	1	10. The Twist	Chubby Checker
				re-entry of 1960 hit (POS 1)	
437	4/07	2	1	11. Johnny Angel	Shelley Fabares
452	11/03	2	1	12. He's A Rebel	The Crystals
524	8/11	2	1	13. Breaking Up Is Hard To Do	Neil Sedaka
529	10/20	2	1	14. Monster Mash	Bobby "Boris" Pickett
533	4/21	2	1	15. Good Luck Charm	Elvis Presley
583	9/01	2	1	16. Sheila	Tommy Roe
628	5/26	1	1	17. Stranger On The Shore	Mr. Acker Bilk
680	7/07	1	1	18. The Stripper	David Rose
795	8/25	1	1	19. The Loco-Motion	Little Eva
895	3/31	1	1	20. Don't Break The Heart That Loves You	Connie Francis
953	11/17	5	2	21. Return To Sender	Elvis Presley
	12/22	2	2	22. Limbo Rock	Chubby Checker
	5/05	2	2	23. Mashed Potato Time	Dee Dee Sharp
	9/22	2	2	24. Ramblin' Rose	Nat King Cole
	7/21	2	2	25. The Wah Watusi	The Orlons
	2/03	1	2	26. Can't Help Falling In Love	Elvis Presley
	2/24	1	2	27. The Wanderer	Dion
	3/17	1	2	28. Midnight In Moscow	Kenny Ball
	9/08	1	2	29. You Don't Know Me	Ray Charles
	11/03	1	2	30. Only Love Can Break A Heart	Gene Pitney
	12/01	4	3	31. Bobby's Girl	Marcie Blane
	10/20	3	3	32. Do You Love Me	The Contours
	11/10	2	3	33. All Alone Am I	Brenda Lee
	6/23	2	3	34. Palisades Park	Freddy Cannon
	7/28	2	3	35. Sealed With A Kiss	Brian Hyland
	4/14	1	3	36. Slow Twistin'	Chubby Checker (with Dee Dee Sharp)
	2/24	1	3	37. Norman	Sue Thompson
	9/29	1	3	38. Green Onions	Booker T. & The MG's
	6/16	1	3	39. It Keeps Right On A-Hurtin'	Johnny Tillotson
	1/27	1	3	40. I Know (You Don't Love Me No More)	Barbara George

1963 — Top 40 Hits

RANK	PK DATE	PK WKS	PK POS		TITLE	ARTIST
120	10/12	5	1	1.	Sugar Shack	Jimmy Gilmer & The Fireballs
196	3/30	4	1	2.	He's So Fine	The Chiffons
198	12/07	4	1	3.	Dominique	The Singing Nun
282	2/09	3	1	4.	Hey Paula	Paul & Paula
283	8/31	3	1	5.	My Boyfriend's Back	The Angels
307	9/21	3	1	6.	Blue Velvet	Bobby Vinton
309	6/15	3	1	7.	Sukiyaki	Kyu Sakamoto
313	4/27	3	1	8.	I Will Follow Him	Little Peggy March
337	8/10	3	1	9.	Fingertips - Pt 2	Little Stevie Wonder
339	3/02	3	1	10.	Walk Like A Man	The 4 Seasons
443	1/12	2	1	11.	Go Away Little Girl	Steve Lawrence
528	11/23	2	1	12.	I'm Leaving It Up To You	Dale & Grace
534	7/20	2	1	13.	Surf City	Jan & Dean
535	6/01	2	1	14.	It's My Party	Lesley Gore
536	1/26	2	1	15.	Walk Right In	The Rooftop Singers
540	7/06	2	1	16.	Easier Said Than Done	The Essex
584	5/18	2	1	17.	If You Wanna Be Happy	Jimmy Soul
800	8/03	1	1	18.	So Much In Love	The Tymes
801	11/16	1	1	19.	Deep Purple	Nino Tempo & April Stevens
894	3/23	1	1	20.	Our Day Will Come	Ruby & The Romantics
949	12/14	6	2	21.	Louie Louie	The Kingsmen
983	4/13	4	2	22.	Can't Get Used To Losing You	Andy Williams
	2/23	3	2	23.	Ruby Baby	Dion
	10/12	3	2	24.	Be My Baby	The Ronettes
	8/24	3	2	25.	Hello Mudduh, Hello Fadduh! (A Letter From Camp)	Allan Sherman
	9/28	2	2	26.	Sally, Go 'Round The Roses	The Jaynetts
	8/17	1	2	27.	Blowin' In The Wind	Peter, Paul & Mary
	11/23	1	2	28.	Washington Square	The Village Stompers
	8/10	1	2	29.	Wipe Out	The Surfaris
	3/23	1	2	30.	The End Of The World	Skeeter Davis
	5/11	1	2	31.	Puff (The Magic Dragon)	Peter, Paul & Mary
	9/07	3	3	32.	If I Had A Hammer	Trini Lopez
	3/16	2	3	33.	You're The Reason I'm Living	Bobby Darin
	2/02	2	3	34.	The Night Has A Thousand Eyes	Bobby Vee
	12/07	2	3	35.	Everybody	Tommy Roe
	8/10	2	3	36.	(You're the) Devil In Disguise	Elvis Presley
	6/22	2	3	37.	Hello Stranger	Barbara Lewis
	3/09	1	3	38.	Rhythm Of The Rain	The Cascades
	5/25	1	3	39.	Surfin' U.S.A.	Beach Boys
	6/01	1	3	40.	I Love You Because	Al Martino

RANK	PK DATE	PK WKS	PK POS	TITLE	ARTIST
51	2/01	7	1	1. I Want To Hold Your Hand	The Beatles
131	4/04	5	1	2. Can't Buy Me Love	The Beatles
199	1/04	4	1	3. There! I've Said It Again	Bobby Vinton
212	10/31	4	1	4. Baby Love	The Supremes
296	9/26	3	1	5. Oh, Pretty Woman	Roy Orbison
317	9/05	3	1	6. The House Of The Rising Sun	The Animals
342	6/06	3	1	7. Chapel Of Love	The Dixie Cups
345	12/26	3	1	8. I Feel Fine	The Beatles
392	3/21	2	1	9. She Loves You	The Beatles
434	7/04	2	1	10. I Get Around	The Beach Boys
441	12/19	2	1	11. Come See About Me	The Supremes
442	8/22	2	1	12. Where Did Our Love Go	The Supremes
448	10/17	2	1	13. Do Wah Diddy Diddy	Manfred Mann
480	5/16	2	1	14. My Guy	Mary Wells
489	8/01	2	1	15. A Hard Day's Night	The Beatles
537	7/18	2	1	16. Rag Doll	The 4 Seasons
614	5/09	1	1	17. Hello, Dolly!	Louis Armstrong
679	12/12	1	1	18. Mr. Lonely	Bobby Vinton
724	8/15	1	1	19. Everybody Loves Somebody	Dean Martin
732	6/27	1	1	20. A World Without Love	Peter & Gordon
819	12/05	1	1	21. Ringo	Lorne Greene
889	5/30	1	1	22. Love Me Do	The Beatles
920	11/28	1	1	23. Leader Of The Pack	The Shangri-Las
982	4/04	4	2	24. Twist And Shout	The Beatles
	2/01	3	2	25. You Don't Own Me	Lesley Gore
	10/17	2	2	26. Dancing In The Street	Martha & The Vandellas
	9/19	2	2	27. Bread And Butter	The Newbeats
	7/11	2	2	28. Memphis	Johnny Rivers
	11/07	1	2	29. Last Kiss	J. Frank Wilson & The Cavaliers
	12/12	1	2	30. She's Not There	The Zombies
	7/04	1	2	31. My Boy Lollipop	Millie Small
	5/09	1	2	32. Do You Want To Know A Secret	The Beatles
	2/22	3	3	33. Dawn (Go Away)	The Four Seasons
	4/11	2	3	34. Suspicion	Terry Stafford
	3/14	2	3	35. Please Please Me	The Beatles
	1/11	2	3	36. Popsicles And Icicles	The Murmaids
	2/01	2	3	37. Out Of Limits	The Marketts
	11/21	2	3	38. Come A Little Bit Closer	Jay & The Americans
	6/13	1	3	39. Love Me With All Your Heart (Cuando Calienta El Sol)	Ray Charles Singers
	8/01	1	3	40. The Little Old Lady (From Pasadena)	Jan & Dean

1965 — Top 40 Hits

RANK	PK DATE	PK WKS	PK POS	TITLE	ARTIST
197	7/10	4	1	1. (I Can't Get No) Satisfaction	The Rolling Stones
218	10/09	4	1	2. Yesterday	The Beatles
311	12/04	3	1	3. Turn! Turn! Turn! (To Everything There Is A Season)	The Byrds
344	5/01	3	1	4. Mrs. Brown You've Got A Lovely Daughter	Herman's Hermits
346	8/14	3	1	5. I Got You Babe	Sonny & Cher
353	9/04	3	1	6. Help!	The Beatles
406	6/19	2	1	7. I Can't Help Myself	Four Tops
432	2/06	2	1	8. You've Lost That Lovin' Feelin'	The Righteous Brothers
436	1/23	2	1	9. Downtown	Petula Clark
450	2/20	2	1	10. This Diamond Ring	Gary Lewis & The Playboys
494	3/27	2	1	11. Stop! In The Name Of Love	The Supremes
532	5/29	2	1	12. Help Me, Rhonda	The Beach Boys
585	11/06	2	1	13. Get Off Of My Cloud	The Rolling Stones
591	11/20	2	1	14. I Hear A Symphony	The Supremes
593	4/10	2	1	15. I'm Telling You Now	Freddie & The Dreamers
599	3/13	2	1	16. Eight Days A Week	The Beatles
731	3/06	1	1	17. My Girl	The Temptations
815	10/02	1	1	18. Hang On Sloopy	The McCoys
818	6/26	1	1	19. Mr. Tambourine Man	The Byrds
821	9/25	1	1	20. Eve Of Destruction	Barry McGuire
891	12/25	1	1	21. Over And Over	The Dave Clark Five
897	5/22	1	1	22. Ticket To Ride	The Beatles
898	8/07	1	1	23. I'm Henry VIII, I Am	Herman's Hermits
921	4/24	1	1	24. Game Of Love	Wayne Fontana/Mindbenders
922	6/12	1	1	25. Back In My Arms Again	The Supremes
	10/30	3	2	26. A Lover's Concerto	The Toys
	6/05	2	2	27. Wooly Bully	Sam The Sham & The Pharaohs
	3/27	2	2	28. Can't You Hear My Heartbeat	Herman's Hermits
	9/04	2	2	29. Like A Rolling Stone	Bob Dylan
	10/16	2	2	30. Treat Her Right	Roy Head & The Traits
	5/08	2	2	31. Count Me In	Gary Lewis & The Playboys
	11/20	1	2	32. 1-2-3	Len Barry
	8/21	1	2	33. Save Your Heart For Me	Gary Lewis & The Playboys
	12/18	3	3	34. I Got You (I Feel Good)	James Brown
	3/20	2	3	35. The Birds And The Bees	Jewel Akens
	1/16	2	3	36. Love Potion Number Nine	The Searchers
	1/30	2	3	37. The Name Game	Shirley Ellis
	7/31	2	3	38. What's New Pussycat?	Tom Jones
	8/28	2	3	39. California Girls	The Beach Boys
	12/11	1	3	40. Let's Hang On!	The 4 Seasons

Top 40 Hits   1966

RANK	PK DATE	PK WKS	PK POS		TITLE	ARTIST
52	12/31	7	1	1.	I'm A Believer	The Monkees
129	3/05	5	1	2.	The Ballad Of The Green Berets	SSgt Barry Sadler
266	12/03	3	1	3.	Winchester Cathedral	New Vaudeville Band
314	4/09	3	1	4.	(You're My) Soul And Inspiration	The Righteous Brothers
315	5/07	3	1	5.	Monday, Monday	The Mama's & The Papa's
343	1/08	3	1	6.	We Can Work It Out	The Beatles
347	8/13	3	1	7.	Summer In The City	The Lovin' Spoonful
352	9/24	3	1	8.	Cherish	The Association
492	9/10	2	1	9.	You Can't Hurry Love	The Supremes
495	7/30	2	1	10.	Wild Thing	The Troggs
527	10/15	2	1	11.	Reach Out I'll Be There	Four Tops
543	6/11	2	1	12.	Paint It, Black	The Rolling Stones
587	5/28	2	1	13.	When A Man Loves A Woman	Percy Sledge
588	11/19	2	1	14.	You Keep Me Hangin' On	The Supremes
589	7/16	2	1	15.	Hanky Panky	Tommy James & The Shondells
592	2/05	2	1	16.	My Love	Petula Clark
594	1/01	2	1	17.	The Sounds Of Silence	Simon & Garfunkel
598	6/25	2	1	18.	Paperback Writer	The Beatles
684	10/29	1	1	19.	96 Tears	? & The Mysterians
685	11/05	1	1	20.	Last Train To Clarksville	The Monkees
799	11/12	1	1	21.	Poor Side Of Town	Johnny Rivers
802	2/26	1	1	22.	These Boots Are Made For Walkin'	Nancy Sinatra
803	12/10	1	1	23.	Good Vibrations	The Beach Boys
804	4/30	1	1	24.	Good Lovin'	The Young Rascals
811	7/02	1	1	25.	Strangers In The Night	Frank Sinatra
817	9/03	1	1	26.	Sunshine Superman	Donovan
892	2/19	1	1	27.	Lightnin' Strikes	Lou Christie
981	12/31	4	2	28.	Snoopy Vs. The Red Baron	The Royal Guardsmen
	12/10	3	2	29.	Mellow Yellow	Donovan
	3/19	3	2	30.	19th Nervous Breakdown	The Rolling Stones
	8/06	2	2	31.	Lil' Red Riding Hood	Sam The Sham & The Pharaohs
	4/09	2	2	32.	Daydream	The Lovin' Spoonful
	8/20	2	2	33.	Sunny	Bobby Hebb
	6/11	2	2	34.	Did You Ever Have To Make Up Your Mind?	The Lovin' Spoonful
	5/28	2	2	35.	A Groovy Kind Of Love	The Mindbenders
	1/29	2	2	36.	Barbara Ann	The Beach Boys
	7/09	1	2	37.	Red Rubber Ball	The Cyrkle
	4/23	1	2	38.	Bang Bang (My Baby Shot Me Down)	Cher
	9/17	1	2	39.	Yellow Submarine	The Beatles
	5/21	1	2	40.	Rainy Day Women #12 & 35	Bob Dylan

RANK	PK DATE	PK WKS	PK POS	TITLE	ARTIST
123	10/21	5	1	1. To Sir With Love	Lulu
182	12/02	4	1	2. Daydream Believer	The Monkees
193	7/01	4	1	3. Windy	The Association
194	8/26	4	1	4. Ode To Billie Joe	Bobbie Gentry
200	4/15	4	1	5. Somethin' Stupid	Nancy Sinatra & Frank Sinatra
201	5/20	4	1	6. Groovin'	The Young Rascals
208	9/23	4	1	7. The Letter	The Box Tops
273	7/29	3	1	8. Light My Fire	The Doors
281	3/25	3	1	9. Happy Together	The Turtles
316	12/30	3	1	10. Hello Goodbye	The Beatles
538	6/03	2	1	11. Respect	Aretha Franklin
541	2/18	2	1	12. Kind Of A Drag	The Buckinghams
678	11/25	1	1	13. Incense And Peppermints	Strawberry Alarm Clock
820	3/11	1	1	14. Love Is Here And Now You're Gone	The Supremes
822	3/04	1	1	15. Ruby Tuesday	The Rolling Stones
823	8/19	1	1	16. All You Need Is Love	The Beatles
896	5/13	1	1	17. The Happening	The Supremes
924	3/18	1	1	18. Penny Lane	The Beatles
	12/16	3	2	19. I Heard It Through The Grapevine	Gladys Knight & The Pips
	11/04	3	2	20. Soul Man	Sam & Dave
	3/25	3	2	21. Dedicated To The One I Love	The Mamas & The Papas
	7/08	2	2	22. Little Bit O'Soul	The Music Explosion
	12/02	2	2	23. The Rain, The Park & Other Things	The Cowsills
	2/04	2	2	24. Georgy Girl	The Seekers
	10/07	2	2	25. Never My Love	The Association
	7/29	2	2	26. I Was Made To Love Her	Stevie Wonder
	9/09	2	2	27. Reflections	Diana Ross & The Supremes
	7/22	1	2	28. Can't Take My Eyes Off You	Frankie Valli
	1/28	1	2	29. Tell It Like It Is	Aaron Neville
	5/13	1	2	30. Sweet Soul Music	Arthur Conley
	4/29	1	2	31. A Little Bit Me, A Little Bit You	The Monkees
	9/09	3	3	32. Come Back When You Grow Up	Bobby Vee & The Strangers
	5/27	3	3	33. I Got Rhythm	The Happenings
	11/04	2	3	34. It Must Be Him	Vikki Carr
	8/19	2	3	35. Pleasant Valley Sunday	The Monkees
	3/11	2	3	36. Baby I Need Your Lovin'	Johnny Rivers
	6/17	2	3	37. She'd Rather Be With Me	The Turtles
	4/15	1	3	38. This Is My Song	Petula Clark
	5/27	4	4	39. Release Me (And Let Me Love Again)	Engelbert Humperdinck
	7/01	4	4	40. San Francisco (Be Sure To Wear Flowers In Your Hair)	Scott McKenzie

Top 40 Hits 1968

RANK	PK DATE	PK WKS	PK POS	TITLE	ARTIST
23	9/28	9	1	1. Hey Jude	The Beatles
54	12/14	7	1	2. I Heard It Through The Grapevine	Marvin Gaye
114	2/10	5	1	3. Love Is Blue	Paul Mauriat
121	4/13	5	1	4. Honey	Bobby Goldsboro
126	8/17	5	1	5. People Got To Be Free	The Rascals
165	3/16	4	1	6. (Sittin' On) The Dock Of The Bay	Otis Redding
211	6/22	4	1	7. This Guy's In Love With You	Herb Alpert
338	6/01	3	1	8. Mrs. Robinson	Simon & Garfunkel
388	11/30	2	1	9. Love Child	Diana Ross & The Supremes
439	5/18	2	1	10. Tighten Up	Archie Bell & The Drells
451	8/03	2	1	11. Hello, I Love You	The Doors
478	1/20	2	1	12. Judy In Disguise (With Glasses)	John Fred & His Playboy Band
542	7/20	2	1	13. Grazing In The Grass	Hugh Masekela
686	9/21	1	1	14. Harper Valley P.T.A.	Jeannie C. Riley
806	2/03	1	1	15. Green Tambourine	The Lemon Pipers
984	2/24	4	2	16. (Theme From) Valley Of The Dolls	Dionne Warwick
	4/06	3	2	17. Young Girl	Union Gap feat. Gary Puckett
	11/02	3	2	18. Those Were The Days	Mary Hopkin
	6/29	3	2	19. The Horse	Cliff Nobles & Co.
	8/24	3	2	20. Born To Be Wild	Steppenwolf
	12/28	2	2	21. For Once In My Life	Stevie Wonder
	1/20	2	2	22. Chain Of Fools	Aretha Franklin
	4/27	2	2	23. Cry Like A Baby	The Box Tops
	8/03	2	2	24. Classical Gas	Mason Williams
	7/20	2	2	25. Lady Willpower	Gary Puckett & The Union Gap
	10/26	1	2	26. Little Green Apples	O.C. Smith
	6/01	1	2	27. The Good, The Bad And The Ugly	Hugo Montenegro
	10/19	1	2	28. Fire	Crazy World Of Arthur Brown
	6/22	1	2	29. MacArthur Park	Richard Harris
	7/27	3	3	30. Stoned Soul Picnic	The 5th Dimension
	2/10	3	3	31. Spooky	Classics IV
	7/06	3	3	32. Jumpin' Jack Flash	The Rolling Stones
	8/31	3	3	33. Light My Fire	Jose Feliciano
	5/25	2	3	34. A Beautiful Morning	The Rascals
	3/30	2	3	35. Valleri	The Monkees
	11/30	1	3	36. Magic Carpet Ride	Steppenwolf
	6/15	1	3	37. Mony Mony	Tommy James & The Shondells
	3/09	4	4	38. Simon Says	1910 Fruitgum Co.
	1/13	3	4	39. Woman, Woman	Union Gap feat. Gary Puckett
	2/17	3	4	40. I Wish It Would Rain	The Temptations

1969   Top 40 Hits

RANK	PK DATE	PK WKS	PK POS		TITLE	ARTIST
78	4/12	6	1	1.	Aquarius/Let The Sunshine In (The Flesh Failures)	The 5th Dimension
87	7/12	6	1	2.	In The Year 2525 (Exordium & Terminus)	Zager & Evans
128	5/24	5	1	3.	Get Back	The Beatles with Billy Preston
156	9/20	4	1	4.	Sugar, Sugar	The Archies
166	8/23	4	1	5.	Honky Tonk Women	The Rolling Stones
189	2/15	4	1	6.	Everyday People	Sly & The Family Stone
192	3/15	4	1	7.	Dizzy	Tommy Roe
298	11/08	3	1	8.	Wedding Bell Blues	The 5th Dimension
387	10/18	2	1	9.	I Can't Get Next To You	The Temptations
389	2/01	2	1	10.	Crimson And Clover	Tommy James & The Shondells
477	12/06	2	1	11.	Na Na Hey Hey Kiss Him Goodbye	Steam
488	6/28	2	1	12.	Love Theme From Romeo & Juliet	Henry Mancini
640	12/20	1	1	13.	Leaving On A Jet Plane	Peter, Paul & Mary
667	11/29	1	1	14.	Come Together	The Beatles
671	12/27	1	1	15.	Someday We'll Be Together	Diana Ross & The Supremes
869	11/01	1	1	16.	Suspicious Minds	Elvis Presley
	7/26	3	2	17.	Crystal Blue Persuasion	Tommy James & The Shondells
	3/08	3	2	18.	Proud Mary	Creedence Clearwater Revival
	7/05	3	2	19.	Spinning Wheel	Blood, Sweat & Tears
	8/23	3	2	20.	A Boy Named Sue	Johnny Cash
	4/12	3	2	21.	You've Made Me So Very Happy	Blood, Sweat & Tears
	5/10	2	2	22.	Hair	The Cowsills
	1/11	2	2	23.	I'm Gonna Make You Love Me	Supremes & Temptations
	10/18	2	2	24.	Hot Fun In The Summertime	Sly & The Family Stone
	10/04	2	2	25.	Jean	Oliver
	5/31	2	2	26.	Love (Can Make You Happy)	Mercy
	9/27	1	2	27.	Green River	Creedence Clearwater Revival
	11/22	1	2	28.	Take A Letter Maria	R.B. Greaves
	5/03	1	2	29.	It's Your Thing	The Isley Brothers
	11/29	1	2	30.	And When I Die	Blood, Sweat & Tears
	6/28	1	2	31.	Bad Moon Rising	Creedence Clearwater Revival
	3/29	1	2	32.	Traces	Classics IV Feat. Dennis Yost
	2/22	3	3	33.	Build Me Up Buttercup	The Foundations
	10/04	2	3	34.	Little Woman	Bobby Sherman
	2/01	2	3	35.	Worst That Could Happen	Brooklyn Bridge
	3/29	2	3	36.	Time Of The Season	The Zombies
	7/12	2	3	37.	Good Morning Starshine	Oliver
	11/15	2	3	38.	Something	The Beatles
	1/11	1	3	39.	Wichita Lineman	Glen Campbell
	12/20	1	3	40.	Down On The Corner	Creedence Clearwater Revival

Top 40 Hits   1970

RANK	PK DATE	PK WKS	PK POS	TITLE	ARTIST
85	2/28	6	1	1. Bridge Over Troubled Water	Simon & Garfunkel
107	10/17	5	1	2. I'll Be There	The Jackson 5
148	1/03	4	1	3. Raindrops Keep Fallin' On My Head	B.J. Thomas
164	7/25	4	1	4. (They Long To Be) Close To You	Carpenters
181	12/26	4	1	5. My Sweet Lord	George Harrison
248	11/21	3	1	6. I Think I Love You	The Partridge Family
280	9/19	3	1	7. Ain't No Mountain High Enough	Diana Ross
297	5/09	3	1	8. American Woman	The Guess Who
303	8/29	3	1	9. War	Edwin Starr
393	4/11	2	1	10. Let It Be	The Beatles
404	12/12	2	1	11. The Tears Of A Clown	Smokey Robinson & Miracles
438	7/11	2	1	12. Mama Told Me (Not To Come)	Three Dog Night
445	4/25	2	1	13. ABC	The Jackson 5
446	6/27	2	1	14. The Love You Save	The Jackson 5
530	2/14	2	1	15. Thank You (Falettinme Be Mice Elf Agin)	Sly & The Family Stone
573	5/30	2	1	16. Everything Is Beautiful	Ray Stevens
590	6/13	2	1	17. The Long And Winding Road	The Beatles
646	8/22	1	1	18. Make It With You	Bread
665	1/31	1	1	19. I Want You Back	The Jackson 5
682	2/07	1	1	20. Venus	The Shocking Blue
771	10/10	1	1	21. Cracklin' Rosie	Neil Diamond
977	10/31	4	2	22. We've Only Just Begun	Carpenters
	12/26	2	2	23. One Less Bell To Answer	The 5th Dimension
	6/06	2	2	24. Which Way You Goin' Billy?	The Poppy Family
	3/07	2	2	25. Travelin' Band	Creedence Clearwater Revival
	10/03	1	2	26. Lookin' Out My Back Door	Creedence Clearwater Revival
	2/21	1	2	27. Hey There Lonely Girl	Eddie Holman
	3/21	1	2	28. The Rapper	The Jaggerz
	5/23	1	2	29. Vehicle	The Ides Of March
	6/27	3	3	30. Ball Of Confusion (That's What The World Is Today)	The Temptations
	10/31	3	3	31. Fire And Rain	James Taylor
	4/18	3	3	32. Spirit In The Sky	Norman Greenbaum
	3/28	3	3	33. Instant Karma (We All Shine On)	John Ono Lennon
	12/05	2	3	34. Gypsy Woman	Brian Hyland
	10/03	2	3	35. Candida	Dawn
	10/17	2	3	36. Green-Eyed Lady	Sugarloaf
	8/08	2	3	37. Signed, Sealed, Delivered I'm Yours	Stevie Wonder
	5/30	2	3	38. Love On A Two-Way Street	The Moments
	7/25	1	3	39. Band Of Gold	Freda Payne
	8/22	1	3	40. Spill The Wine	Eric Burdon & War

RANK	PK DATE	PK WKS	PK POS	TITLE	ARTIST
81	4/17	6	1	1. Joy To The World	Three Dog Night
109	10/02	5	1	2. Maggie May	Rod Stewart
115	6/19	5	1	3. It's Too Late	Carole King
127	2/13	5	1	4. One Bad Apple	The Osmonds
178	8/07	4	1	5. How Can You Mend A Broken Heart	The Bee Gees
249	1/23	3	1	6. Knock Three Times	Dawn
265	12/25	3	1	7. Brand New Key	Melanie
278	9/11	3	1	8. Go Away Little Girl	Donny Osmond
279	12/04	3	1	9. Family Affair	Sly & The Family Stone
427	11/06	2	1	10. Gypsys, Tramps & Thieves	Cher
435	4/03	2	1	11. Just My Imagination (Running Away With Me)	The Temptations
447	11/20	2	1	12. Theme From Shaft	Isaac Hayes
486	3/20	2	1	13. Me And Bobby McGee	Janis Joplin
490	5/29	2	1	14. Brown Sugar	The Rolling Stones
669	7/24	1	1	15. Indian Reservation (The Lament Of The Cherokee Reservation Indian)	Raiders
723	6/12	1	1	16. Want Ads	The Honey Cone
729	7/31	1	1	17. You've Got A Friend	James Taylor
805	9/04	1	1	18. Uncle Albert/Admiral Halsey	Paul & Linda McCartney
	4/10	3	2	19. What's Going On	Marvin Gaye
	5/08	3	2	20. Never Can Say Goodbye	The Jackson 5
	8/14	2	2	21. Mr. Big Stuff	Jean Knight
	10/16	2	2	22. Superstar	Carpenters
	6/19	2	2	23. Rainy Days And Mondays	Carpenters
	9/11	2	2	24. Spanish Harlem	Aretha Franklin
	2/27	2	2	25. Mama's Pearl	The Jackson 5
	8/28	1	2	26. Take Me Home, Country Roads	John Denver
	3/20	1	2	27. She's A Lady	Tom Jones
	5/01	1	2	28. Put Your Hand In The Hand	Ocean
	10/16	3	3	29. Yo-Yo	The Osmonds
	12/11	2	3	30. Have You Seen Her	Chi-Lites
	7/03	2	3	31. Treat Her Like A Lady	Cornelius Brothers & Sister Rose
	3/13	2	3	32. For All We Know	Carpenters
	2/13	2	3	33. Rose Garden	Lynn Anderson
	9/04	2	3	34. Smiling Faces Sometimes	The Undisputed Truth
	9/18	2	3	35. Ain't No Sunshine	Bill Withers
	11/13	2	3	36. Imagine	John Lennon
	11/27	2	3	37. Baby I'm-A Want You	Bread
	10/02	1	3	38. The Night They Drove Old Dixie Down	Joan Baez
	1/30	1	3	39. Lonely Days	Bee Gees
	8/28	1	3	40. Signs	Five Man Electrical Band

Top 40 Hits   1972

RANK	PK DATE	PK WKS	PK POS	TITLE	ARTIST
79	4/15	6	1	1. The First Time Ever I Saw Your Face	Roberta Flack
80	7/29	6	1	2. Alone Again (Naturally)	Gilbert O'Sullivan
163	1/15	4	1	3. American Pie - Parts I & II	Don McLean
190	2/19	4	1	4. Without You	Nilsson
205	11/04	4	1	5. I Can See Clearly Now	Johnny Nash
267	3/25	3	1	6. A Horse With No Name	America
277	9/23	3	1	7. Baby Don't Get Hooked On Me	Mac Davis
295	12/16	3	1	8. Me And Mrs. Jones	Billy Paul
321	6/10	3	1	9. The Candy Man	Sammy Davis, Jr.
326	7/08	3	1	10. Lean On Me	Bill Withers
580	10/21	2	1	11. My Ding-A-Ling	Chuck Berry
644	8/26	1	1	12. Brandy (You're A Fine Girl)	Looking Glass
672	2/12	1	1	13. Let's Stay Together	Al Green
710	12/09	1	1	14. I Am Woman	Helen Reddy
719	6/03	1	1	15. I'll Take You There	The Staple Singers
726	3/18	1	1	16. Heart Of Gold	Neil Young
772	5/27	1	1	17. Oh Girl	Chi-Lites
808	10/14	1	1	18. Ben	Michael Jackson
882	12/02	1	1	19. Papa Was A Rollin' Stone	The Temptations
885	7/01	1	1	20. Song Sung Blue	Neil Diamond
923	9/16	1	1	21. Black & White	Three Dog Night
	5/06	2	2	22. I Gotcha	Joe Tex
	9/02	2	2	23. Long Cool Woman (In A Black Dress)	The Hollies
	7/15	2	2	24. Too Late To Turn Back Now	Cornelius Brothers & Sister Rose
	4/22	2	2	25. Rockin' Robin	Michael Jackson
	11/04	2	2	26. Nights In White Satin	The Moody Blues
	12/30	2	2	27. Clair	Gilbert O'Sullivan
	2/26	2	2	28. Hurting Each Other	Carpenters
	11/18	2	2	29. I'd Love You To Want Me	Lobo
	10/14	2	2	30. Use Me	Bill Withers
	7/08	1	2	31. Outa-Space	Billy Preston
	10/28	1	2	32. Burning Love	Elvis Presley
	3/11	3	3	33. The Lion Sleeps Tonight	Robert John
	8/05	2	3	34. (If Loving You Is Wrong) I Don't Want To Be Right	Luther Ingram
	2/26	2	3	35. Precious And Few	Climax
	12/23	2	3	36. You Ought To Be With Me	Al Green
	9/02	2	3	37. I'm Still In Love With You	Al Green
	12/09	2	3	38. If You Don't Know Me By Now	Harold Melvin & The Bluenotes
	11/18	2	3	39. I'll Be Around	The Spinners
	9/23	2	3	40. Saturday In The Park	Chicago

1973 — Top 40 Hits

RANK	PK DATE	PK WKS	PK POS	TITLE	ARTIST
125	2/24	5	1	1. Killing Me Softly With His Song	Roberta Flack
162	4/21	4	1	2. Tie A Yellow Ribbon Round The Ole Oak Tree	Dawn Feat. Tony Orlando
188	6/02	4	1	3. My Love	Paul McCartney & Wings
251	1/06	3	1	4. You're So Vain	Carly Simon
275	2/03	3	1	5. Crocodile Rock	Elton John
374	9/08	2	1	6. Let's Get It On	Marvin Gaye
400	11/10	2	1	7. Keep On Truckin' (Part 1)	Eddie Kendricks
455	7/21	2	1	8. Bad, Bad Leroy Brown	Jim Croce
458	12/01	2	1	9. Top Of The World	Carpenters
459	10/27	2	1	10. Midnight Train To Georgia	Gladys Knight & The Pips
466	8/25	2	1	11. Brother Louie	Stories
469	7/07	2	1	12. Will It Go Round In Circles	Billy Preston
471	10/06	2	1	13. Half-Breed	Cher
512	4/07	2	1	14. The Night The Lights Went Out In Georgia	Vicki Lawrence
526	12/29	2	1	15. Time In A Bottle	Jim Croce
544	12/15	2	1	16. The Most Beautiful Girl	Charlie Rich
582	8/04	2	1	17. The Morning After	Maureen McGovern
694	8/18	1	1	18. Touch Me In The Morning	Diana Ross
715	9/15	1	1	19. Delta Dawn	Helen Reddy
763	5/26	1	1	20. Frankenstein	The Edgar Winter Group
784	5/19	1	1	21. You Are The Sunshine Of My Life	Stevie Wonder
787	10/20	1	1	22. Angie	The Rolling Stones
814	6/30	1	1	23. Give Me Love - (Give Me Peace On Earth)	George Harrison
864	9/29	1	1	24. We're An American Band	Grand Funk
866	1/27	1	1	25. Superstition	Stevie Wonder
870	3/24	1	1	26. Love Train	O'Jays
880	11/24	1	1	27. Photograph	Ringo Starr
986	2/24	4	2	28. Dueling Banjos	Eric Weissberg & Steve Mandell
	12/08	3	2	29. Goodbye Yellow Brick Road	Elton John
	8/11	3	2	30. Live And Let Die	Wings
	6/16	2	2	31. Playground In My Mind	Clint Holmes
	7/07	2	2	32. Kodachrome	Paul Simon
	4/07	2	2	33. Neither One Of Us (Wants To Be The First To Say Goodbye)	Gladys Knight & The Pips
	4/28	2	2	34. The Cisco Kid	War
	10/06	1	2	35. Loves Me Like A Rock	Paul Simon
	6/02	1	2	36. Daniel	Elton John
	10/13	1	2	37. Ramblin Man	The Allman Brothers Band
	7/28	1	2	38. Yesterday Once More	Carpenters
	3/31	1	2	39. Also Sprach Zarathustra (2001)	Deodato
	5/05	3	3	40. Little Willy	The Sweet

Top 40 Hits   1974

RANK	PK DATE	PK WKS	PK POS	TITLE	ARTIST
269	2/02	3	1	1. The Way We Were	Barbra Streisand
287	3/02	3	1	2. Seasons In The Sun	Terry Jacks
306	5/18	3	1	3. The Streak	Ray Stevens
354	8/24	3	1	4. (You're) Having My Baby	Paul Anka with Odia Coates
483	12/07	2	1	5. Kung Fu Fighting	Carl Douglas
523	6/15	2	1	6. Billy, Don't Be A Hero	Bo Donaldson & The Heywoods
531	7/27	2	1	7. Annie's Song	John Denver
556	5/04	2	1	8. The Loco-Motion	Grand Funk
561	4/20	2	1	9. TSOP (The Sound Of Philadelphia)	MFSB with The Three Degrees
578	11/23	2	1	10. I Can Help	Billy Swan
596	7/13	2	1	11. Rock Your Baby	George McCrae
597	10/05	2	1	12. I Honestly Love You	Olivia Newton-John
666	4/13	1	1	13. Bennie And The Jets	Elton John
696	1/12	1	1	14. The Joker	Steve Miller Band
706	10/26	1	1	15. Then Came You	Dionne Warwicke & the Spinners
737	2/09	1	1	16. Love's Theme	Love Unlimited Orchestra
738	1/19	1	1	17. Show And Tell	Al Wilson
764	11/02	1	1	18. You Haven't Done Nothin	Stevie Wonder
767	10/19	1	1	19. Nothing From Nothing	Billy Preston
770	4/06	1	1	20. Hooked On A Feeling	Blue Swede
781	3/30	1	1	21. Sunshine On My Shoulders	John Denver
782	6/08	1	1	22. Band On The Run	Paul McCartney & Wings
797	1/26	1	1	23. You're Sixteen	Ringo Starr
807	6/29	1	1	24. Sundown	Gordon Lightfoot
860	9/28	1	1	25. Rock Me Gently	Andy Kim
863	12/28	1	1	26. Angie Baby	Helen Reddy
867	8/10	1	1	27. Feel Like Makin' Love	Roberta Flack
874	12/21	1	1	28. Cat's In The Cradle	Harry Chapin
881	3/23	1	1	29. Dark Lady	Cher
887	8/17	1	1	30. The Night Chicago Died	Paper Lace
911	11/09	1	1	31. You Ain't Seen Nothing Yet	Bachman-Turner Overdrive
916	7/06	1	1	32. Rock The Boat	The Hues Corporation
918	9/14	1	1	33. I Shot The Sheriff	Eric Clapton
931	9/21	1	1	34. Can't Get Enough Of Your Love, Babe	Barry White
932	11/16	1	1	35. Whatever Gets You Thru The Night	John Lennon
	5/18	2	2	36. Dancing Machine	The Jackson 5
	6/15	2	2	37. You Make Me Feel Brand New	The Stylistics
	11/16	2	2	38. Do It ('Til You're Satisfied)	B.T. Express
	3/09	2	2	39. Boogie Down	Eddie Kendricks
	7/27	2	2	40. Don't Let The Sun Go Down On Me	Elton John

1975 — Top 40 Hits

RANK	PK DATE	PK WKS	PK POS	TITLE	ARTIST
216	6/21	4	1	1. Love Will Keep Us Together	The Captain & Tennille
332	11/29	3	1	2. Fly, Robin, Fly	Silver Convention
336	11/01	3	1	3. Island Girl	Elton John
355	5/03	3	1	4. He Don't Love You (Like I Love You)	Tony Orlando & Dawn
356	10/11	3	1	5. Bad Blood	Neil Sedaka
410	9/06	2	1	6. Rhinestone Cowboy	Glen Campbell
415	4/12	2	1	7. Philadelphia Freedom	The Elton John Band
433	11/22	2	1	8. That's The Way (I Like It)	KC & The Sunshine Band
484	8/09	2	1	9. Jive Talkin'	Bee Gees
555	9/20	2	1	10. Fame	David Bowie
586	1/04	2	1	11. Lucy In The Sky With Diamonds	Elton John
643	8/02	1	1	12. One Of These Nights	Eagles
702	5/31	1	1	13. Before The Next Teardrop Falls	Freddy Fender
708	3/22	1	1	14. My Eyes Adored You	Frankie Valli
722	4/05	1	1	15. Lovin' You	Minnie Riperton
750	2/01	1	1	16. Laughter In The Rain	Neil Sedaka
768	4/26	1	1	17. (Hey Won't You Play) Another Somebody Done Somebody Wrong Song	B.J. Thomas
783	3/29	1	1	18. Lady Marmalade	LaBelle
785	2/22	1	1	19. Pick Up The Pieces	AWB
793	7/26	1	1	20. The Hustle	Van McCoy
794	3/15	1	1	21. Black Water	The Doobie Brothers
798	12/27	1	1	22. Let's Do It Again	The Staple Singers
809	3/08	1	1	23. Have You Never Been Mellow	Olivia Newton-John
812	7/19	1	1	24. Listen To What The Man Said	Wings
849	3/01	1	1	25. Best Of My Love	The Eagles
878	8/23	1	1	26. Fallin' In Love	Hamilton, Joe Frank & Reynolds
900	6/07	1	1	27. Thank God I'm A Country Boy	John Denver
901	5/24	1	1	28. Shining Star	Earth, Wind & Fire
912	1/25	1	1	29. Please Mr. Postman	Carpenters
913	1/18	1	1	30. Mandy	Barry Manilow
917	2/15	1	1	31. You're No Good	Linda Ronstadt
926	9/27	1	1	32. I'm Sorry	John Denver
927	2/08	1	1	33. Fire	Ohio Players
928	6/14	1	1	34. Sister Golden Hair	America
930	8/30	1	1	35. Get Down Tonight	K.C. & The Sunshine Band
987	10/11	4	2	36. Calypso	John Denver
	7/26	3	2	37. I'm Not In Love	10cc
	6/21	2	2	38. When Will I Be Loved	Linda Ronstadt
	1/04	2	2	39. You're The First, The Last, My Everything	Barry White
	11/08	2	2	40. Lyin' Eyes	The Eagles

Top 40 Hits   1976

RANK	PK DATE	PK WKS	PK POS	TITLE	ARTIST
37	11/13	8	1	1. Tonight's The Night (Gonna Be Alright)	Rod Stewart
108	5/22	5	1	2. Silly Love Songs	Wings
204	8/07	4	1	3. Don't Go Breaking My Heart	Elton John & Kiki Dee
207	4/03	4	1	4. Disco Lady	Johnnie Taylor
254	9/18	3	1	5. Play That Funky Music	Wild Cherry
350	3/13	3	1	6. December, 1963 (Oh, What a Night)	The Four Seasons
351	2/07	3	1	7. 50 Ways To Leave Your Lover	Paul Simon
411	7/24	2	1	8. Kiss And Say Goodbye	Manhattans
416	10/23	2	1	9. If You Leave Me Now	Chicago
429	5/29	2	1	10. Love Hangover	Diana Ross
474	7/10	2	1	11. Afternoon Delight	Starland Vocal Band
626	9/11	1	1	12. (Shake, Shake, Shake) Shake Your Booty	K.C. & The Sunshine Band
630	10/09	1	1	13. A Fifth Of Beethoven	Walter Murphy
635	10/16	1	1	14. Disco Duck (Part 1)	Rick Dees & His Cast Of Idiots
638	1/17	1	1	15. I Write The Songs	Barry Manilow
645	1/31	1	1	16. Love Rollercoaster	Ohio Players
747	5/15	1	1	17. Boogie Fever	Sylvers
786	1/24	1	1	18. Theme From Mahogany (Do You Know Where You're Going To)	Diana Ross
790	9/04	1	1	19. You Should Be Dancing	Bee Gees
792	5/01	1	1	20. Let Your Love Flow	Bellamy Brothers
810	1/10	1	1	21. Convoy	C.W. McCall
813	5/08	1	1	22. Welcome Back	John Sebastian
824	3/06	1	1	23. Love Machine (Part 1)	The Miracles
871	2/28	1	1	24. Theme From S.W.A.T.	Rhythm Heritage
876	1/03	1	1	25. Saturday Night	Bay City Rollers
902	11/06	1	1	26. Rock'n Me	Steve Miller
	12/04	3	2	27. The Rubberband Man	The Spinners
	6/12	3	2	28. Get Up And Boogie (That's Right)	Silver Convention
	3/27	3	2	29. Dream Weaver	Gary Wright
	3/06	3	2	30. All By Myself	Eric Carmen
	9/25	2	2	31. I'd Really Love To See You Tonight	England Dan & John Ford Coley
	5/01	2	2	32. Right Back Where We Started From	Maxine Nightingale
	9/04	2	2	33. You'll Never Find Another Love Like Mine	Lou Rawls
	7/31	2	2	34. Love Is Alive	Gary Wright
	2/07	2	2	35. Love To Love You Baby	Donna Summer
	11/20	2	2	36. The Wreck Of The Edmund Fitzgerald	Gordon Lightfoot
	11/20	4	3	37. Love So Right	Bee Gees
	6/12	4	3	38. Misty Blue	Dorothy Moore
	8/14	4	3	39. Let 'Em In	Wings
	2/07	3	3	40. You Sexy Thing	Hot Chocolate

RANK	PK DATE	PK WKS	PK POS	TITLE	ARTIST
19	10/15	10	1	1. You Light Up My Life	Debby Boone
102	8/20	5	1	2. Best Of My Love	Emotions
141	7/30	4	1	3. I Just Want To Be Your Everything	Andy Gibb
222	12/24	3	1	4. How Deep Is Your Love	Bee Gees
231	3/05	3	1	5. Love Theme From "A Star Is Born" (Evergreen)	Barbra Streisand
301	5/21	3	1	6. Sir Duke	Stevie Wonder
397	2/05	2	1	7. Torn Between Two Lovers	Mary MacGregor
559	3/26	2	1	8. Rich Girl	Daryl Hall & John Oates
567	10/01	2	1	9. Star Wars Theme/Cantina Band	Meco
670	6/25	1	1	10. Got To Give It Up (Pt. I)	Marvin Gaye
674	1/29	1	1	11. Car Wash	Rose Royce
687	1/08	1	1	12. You Don't Have To Be A Star (To Be In My Show)	Marilyn McCoo & Billy Davis, Jr.
691	4/23	1	1	13. Don't Leave Me This Way	Thelma Houston
692	1/15	1	1	14. You Make Me Feel Like Dancing	Leo Sayer
698	4/09	1	1	15. Dancing Queen	Abba
703	4/30	1	1	16. Southern Nights	Glen Campbell
704	2/19	1	1	17. Blinded By The Light	Manfred Mann's Earth Band
705	5/07	1	1	18. Hotel California	Eagles
707	1/22	1	1	19. I Wish	Stevie Wonder
720	7/02	1	1	20. Gonna Fly Now	Bill Conti
735	7/09	1	1	21. Undercover Angel	Alan O'Day
761	5/14	1	1	22. When I Need You	Leo Sayer
778	4/16	1	1	23. Don't Give Up On Us	David Soul
780	6/18	1	1	24. Dreams	Fleetwood Mac
788	2/26	1	1	25. New Kid In Town	Eagles
789	7/16	1	1	26. Da Doo Ron Ron	Shaun Cassidy
826	6/11	1	1	27. I'm Your Boogie Man	KC & The Sunshine Band
906	7/23	1	1	28. Looks Like We Made It	Barry Manilow
	11/26	3	2	29. Don't It Make My Brown Eyes Blue	Crystal Gayle
	10/22	3	2	30. Nobody Does It Better	Carly Simon
	10/01	3	2	31. Keep It Comin' Love	KC & The Sunshine Band
	7/30	3	2	32. I'm In You	Peter Frampton
	11/12	2	2	33. Boogie Nights	Heatwave
	3/12	2	2	34. Fly Like An Eagle	Steve Miller
	9/17	2	2	35. Float On	The Floaters
	9/10	1	2	36. (Your Love Has Lifted Me) Higher And Higher	Rita Coolidge
	12/17	4	3	37. Blue Bayou	Linda Ronstadt
	1/29	2	3	38. Dazz	Brick
	10/22	2	3	39. That's Rock 'N' Roll	Shaun Cassidy
	9/24	2	3	40. Don't Stop	Fleetwood Mac

RANK	PK DATE	PK WKS	PK POS	TITLE	ARTIST
35	3/18	8	1	1. Night Fever	Bee Gees
46	6/17	7	1	2. Shadow Dancing	Andy Gibb
65	12/09	6	1	3. Le Freak	Chic
147	2/04	4	1	4. Stayin' Alive	Bee Gees
158	9/30	4	1	5. Kiss You All Over	Exile
240	9/09	3	1	6. Boogie Oogie Oogie	A Taste Of Honey
256	1/14	3	1	7. Baby Come Back	Player
272	11/11	3	1	8. MacArthur Park	Donna Summer
380	3/04	2	1	9. (Love Is) Thicker Than Water	Andy Gibb
385	8/12	2	1	10. Three Times A Lady	Commodores
401	12/02	2	1	11. You Don't Bring Me Flowers	Barbra & Neil
461	8/26	2	1	12. Grease	Frankie Valli
482	5/20	2	1	13. With A Little Luck	Wings
636	5/13	1	1	14. If I Can't Have You	Yvonne Elliman
650	10/28	1	1	15. Hot Child In The City	Nick Gilder
657	6/10	1	1	16. You're The One That I Want	John Travolta & Olivia Newton-John
664	8/05	1	1	17. Miss You	The Rolling Stones
689	11/04	1	1	18. You Needed Me	Anne Murray
730	6/03	1	1	19. Too Much, Too Little, Too Late	Johnny Mathis/ Deniece Williams
948	6/24	6	2	20. Baker Street	Gerry Rafferty
	1/28	3	2	21. Short People	Randy Newman
	5/13	2	2	22. The Closer I Get To You	Roberta Flack/Donny Hathaway
	11/18	2	2	23. Double Vision	Foreigner
	4/01	3	3	24. Lay Down Sally	Eric Clapton
	4/22	3	3	25. Can't Smile Without You	Barry Manilow
	11/18	3	3	26. How Much I Feel	Ambrosia
	3/18	2	3	27. Emotion	Samantha Sang
	2/18	2	3	28. Just The Way You Are	Billy Joel
	3/04	2	3	29. Sometimes When We Touch	Dan Hill
	9/23	2	3	30. Hopelessly Devoted To You	Olivia Newton-John
	7/08	2	3	31. Take A Chance On Me	Abba
	9/09	2	3	32. Hot Blooded	Foreigner
	8/12	2	3	33. Last Dance	Donna Summer
	10/28	2	3	34. Reminiscing	Little River Band
	6/24	2	3	35. It's A Heartache	Bonnie Tyler
	1/14	2	3	36. Here You Come Again	Dolly Parton
	2/04	3	4	37. We Are The Champions	Queen
	1/14	3	4	38. You're In My Heart (The Final Acclaim)	Rod Stewart
	12/09	2	4	39. I Just Wanna Stop	Gino Vannelli
	7/08	2	4	40. Use Ta Be My Girl	The O'Jays

RANK	PK DATE	PK WKS	PK POS		TITLE	ARTIST
77	8/25	6	1	1.	My Sharona	The Knack
113	7/14	5	1	2.	Bad Girls	Donna Summer
157	2/10	4	1	3.	Da Ya Think I'm Sexy?	Rod Stewart
171	5/05	4	1	4.	Reunited	Peaches & Herb
230	6/02	3	1	5.	Hot Stuff	Donna Summer
232	3/10	3	1	6.	I Will Survive	Gloria Gaynor
258	12/22	3	1	7.	Escape (The Pina Colada Song)	Rupert Holmes
386	6/30	2	1	8.	Ring My Bell	Anita Ward
391	12/08	2	1	9.	Babe	Styx
417	1/06	2	1	10.	Too Much Heaven	Bee Gees
421	10/20	2	1	11.	Rise	Herb Alpert
428	3/24	2	1	12.	Tragedy	Bee Gees
440	11/24	2	1	13.	No More Tears (Enough Is Enough)	Barbra Streisand/ Donna Summer
617	11/17	1	1	14.	Still	Commodores
648	11/03	1	1	15.	Pop Muzik	M
649	10/06	1	1	16.	Sad Eyes	Robert John
676	4/14	1	1	17.	What A Fool Believes	The Doobie Brothers
677	8/18	1	1	18.	Good Times	Chic
681	11/10	1	1	19.	Heartache Tonight	Eagles
757	4/28	1	1	20.	Heart Of Glass	Blondie
844	4/21	1	1	21.	Knock On Wood	Amii Stewart
873	10/13	1	1	22.	Don't Stop 'Til You Get Enough	Michael Jackson
907	6/09	1	1	23.	Love You Inside Out	Bee Gees
999	2/03	3	2	24.	Y.M.C.A.	Village People
	11/10	2	2	25.	Dim All The Lights	Donna Summer
	9/15	2	2	26.	After The Love Has Gone	Earth, Wind & Fire
	2/24	2	2	27.	Fire	Pointer Sisters
	6/16	2	2	28.	We Are Family	Sister Sledge
	8/11	4	3	29.	The Main Event/Fight	Barbra Streisand
	1/06	3	3	30.	My Life	Billy Joel
	2/17	2	3	31.	A Little More Love	Olivia Newton-John
	9/15	2	3	32.	The Devil Went Down To Georgia	The Charlie Daniels Band
	5/19	2	3	33.	In The Navy	Village People
	5/05	1	3	34.	Music Box Dancer	Frank Mills
	12/22	4	4	35.	Send One Your Love	Stevie Wonder
	3/17	3	4	36.	Heaven Knows	Donna Summer with Brooklyn Dreams
	5/12	2	4	37.	Stumblin' In	Suzi Quatro & Chris Norman
	10/13	2	4	38.	Sail On	Commodores
	4/07	2	4	39.	Sultans Of Swing	Dire Straits
	6/16	2	4	40.	Just When I Needed You Most	Randy Vanwarmer

Top 40 Hits

1980

RANK	PK DATE	PK WKS	PK POS	TITLE	ARTIST
70	11/15	6	1	1. Lady	Kenny Rogers
75	4/19	6	1	2. Call Me	Blondie
97	12/27	5	1	3. (Just Like) Starting Over	John Lennon
145	9/06	4	1	4. Upside Down	Diana Ross
154	3/22	4	1	5. Another Brick In The Wall (Part II)	Pink Floyd
159	2/23	4	1	6. Crazy Little Thing Called Love	Queen
183	1/19	4	1	7. Rock With You	Michael Jackson
184	8/02	4	1	8. Magic	Olivia Newton-John
186	5/31	4	1	9. Funkytown	Lipps, Inc.
226	10/04	3	1	10. Another One Bites The Dust	Queen
243	10/25	3	1	11. Woman In Love	Barbra Streisand
247	6/28	3	1	12. Coming Up (Live at Glasgow)	Paul McCartney & Wings
383	7/19	2	1	13. It's Still Rock And Roll To Me	Billy Joel
610	2/16	1	1	14. Do That To Me One More Time	The Captain & Tennille
624	1/05	1	1	15. Please Don't Go	K.C. & The Sunshine Band
775	8/30	1	1	16. Sailing	Christopher Cross
954	12/06	5	2	17. More Than I Can Say	Leo Sayer
970	9/13	4	2	18. All Out Of Love	Air Supply
974	4/26	4	2	19. Ride Like The Wind	Christopher Cross
	3/29	2	2	20. Working My Way Back To You/ Forgive Me, Girl	Spinners
	3/01	2	2	21. Yes, I'm Ready	Teri DeSario with K.C.
	3/15	2	2	22. Longer	Dan Fogelberg
	7/19	4	3	23. Little Jeannie	Elton John
	1/26	4	3	24. Coward Of The County	Kenny Rogers
	5/03	4	3	25. Lost In Love	Air Supply
	6/28	3	3	26. The Rose	Bette Midler
	6/07	3	3	27. Biggest Part Of Me	Ambrosia
	11/15	3	3	28. The Wanderer	Donna Summer
	10/25	3	3	29. He's So Shy	Pointer Sisters
	9/06	2	3	30. Emotional Rescue	The Rolling Stones
	8/16	2	3	31. Take Your Time (Do It Right) Part 1	The S.O.S. Band
	3/08	4	4	32. Desire	Andy Gibb
	2/02	4	4	33. Cruisin'	Smokey Robinson
	4/19	4	4	34. With You I'm Born Again	Billy Preston & Syreeta
	7/19	3	4	35. Cupid/I've Loved You For A Long Time	Spinners
	5/24	3	4	36. Don't Fall In Love With A Dreamer	Kenny Rogers with Kim Carnes
	9/27	2	4	37. Give Me The Night	George Benson
	9/13	2	4	38. Fame	Irene Cara
	12/27	5	5	39. Hungry Heart	Bruce Springsteen
	12/06	3	5	40. Master Blaster (Jammin')	Stevie Wonder

RANK	PK DATE	PK WKS	PK POS	TITLE	ARTIST
18	11/21	10	1	1. Physical	Olivia Newton-John
22	5/16	9	1	2. Bette Davis Eyes	Kim Carnes
24	8/15	9	1	3. Endless Love	Diana Ross & Lionel Richie
239	10/17	3	1	4. Arthur's Theme (Best That You Can Do)	Christopher Cross
285	4/11	3	1	5. Kiss On My List	Daryl Hall & John Oates
377	8/01	2	1	6. Jessie's Girl	Rick Springfield
408	2/28	2	1	7. I Love A Rainy Night	Eddie Rabbitt
409	2/21	2	1	8. 9 To 5	Dolly Parton
414	11/07	2	1	9. Private Eyes	Daryl Hall & John Oates
473	3/28	2	1	10. Rapture	Blondie
496	2/07	2	1	11. Celebration	Kool & The Gang
549	5/02	2	1	12. Morning Train (Nine To Five)	Sheena Easton
634	1/31	1	1	13. The Tide Is High	Blondie
647	3/21	1	1	14. Keep On Loving You	REO Speedwagon
711	6/20	1	1	15. Medley	Stars on 45
718	7/25	1	1	16. The One That You Love	Air Supply
933	11/28	10	2	17. Waiting For A Girl Like You	Foreigner
	3/21	3	2	18. Woman	John Lennon
	10/31	3	2	19. Start Me Up	The Rolling Stones
	8/29	3	2	20. Slow Hand	Pointer Sisters
	5/02	3	2	21. Just The Two Of Us	Grover Washington, Jr. (with Bill Withers)
	1/10	3	2	22. Love On The Rocks	Neil Diamond
	5/23	3	2	23. Being With You	Smokey Robinson
	7/04	3	2	24. All Those Years Ago	George Harrison
	9/19	2	2	25. Queen Of Hearts	Juice Newton
	8/15	2	2	26. Theme From "Greatest American Hero" (Believe It or Not)	Joey Scarbury
	9/05	6	3	27. Stop Draggin' My Heart Around	Stevie Nicks (with Tom Petty & The Heartbreakers)
	12/19	5	3	28. Let's Groove	Earth, Wind & Fire
	3/21	4	3	29. The Best Of Times	Styx
	6/13	3	3	30. Sukiyaki	A Taste Of Honey
	8/15	2	3	31. I Don't Need You	Kenny Rogers
	1/10	2	3	32. Guilty	Barbra Streisand & Barry Gibb
	12/05	2	3	33. Every Little Thing She Does Is Magic	The Police
	9/05	4	4	34. Urgent	Foreigner
	5/02	4	4	35. Angel Of The Morning	Juice Newton
	10/17	4	4	36. For Your Eyes Only	Sheena Easton
	12/05	3	4	37. Oh No	Commodores
	10/03	2	4	38. Who's Crying Now	Journey
	6/20	2	4	39. A Woman Needs Love (Just Like You Do)	Ray Parker Jr. & Raydio
	9/05	5	5	40. (There's) No Gettin' Over Me	Ronnie Milsap

RANK	PK DATE	PK WKS	PK POS	TITLE	ARTIST
49	3/20	7	1	1. I Love Rock 'N Roll	Joan Jett & The Blackhearts
50	5/15	7	1	2. Ebony And Ivory	Paul McCartney/Stevie Wonder
67	7/24	6	1	3. Eye Of The Tiger	Survivor
74	2/06	6	1	4. Centerfold	The J. Geils Band
150	12/18	4	1	5. Maneater	Daryl Hall & John Oates
169	10/02	4	1	6. Jack & Diane	John Cougar
235	7/03	3	1	7. Don't You Want Me	The Human League
322	11/06	3	1	8. Up Where We Belong	Joe Cocker & Jennifer Warnes
370	9/04	2	1	9. Abracadabra	The Steve Miller Band
379	9/11	2	1	10. Hard To Say I'm Sorry	Chicago
405	11/27	2	1	11. Truly	Lionel Richie
621	1/30	1	1	12. I Can't Go For That (No Can Do)	Daryl Hall & John Oates
632	12/11	1	1	13. Mickey	Toni Basil
652	10/30	1	1	14. Who Can It Be Now?	Men At Work
668	5/08	1	1	15. Chariots Of Fire - Titles	Vangelis
947	2/27	6	2	16. Open Arms	Journey
952	7/03	5	2	17. Rosanna	Toto
960	8/07	4	2	18. Hurts So Good	John Cougar
968	5/22	4	2	19. Don't Talk To Strangers	Rick Springfield
	11/27	3	2	20. Gloria	Laura Branigan
	4/10	3	2	21. We Got The Beat	Go-Go's
	11/06	4	3	22. Heart Attack	Olivia Newton-John
	10/16	3	3	23. Eye In The Sky	The Alan Parsons Project
	5/22	3	3	24. I've Never Been To Me	Charlene
	2/13	2	3	25. Harden My Heart	Quarterflash
	7/24	7	4	26. Hold Me	Fleetwood Mac
	4/10	4	4	27. Freeze-Frame	The J. Geils Band
	3/20	3	4	28. That Girl	Stevie Wonder
	5/22	3	4	29. 867-5309/Jenny	Tommy Tutone
	2/27	3	4	30. Shake It Up	The Cars
	10/23	3	4	31. I Keep Forgettin' (Every Time You're Near)	Michael McDonald
	6/26	3	4	32. Heat Of The Moment	Asia
	6/12	2	4	33. The Other Woman	Ray Parker Jr.
	11/13	4	5	34. Heartlight	Neil Diamond
	6/12	3	5	35. Always On My Mind	Willie Nelson
	9/18	3	5	36. You Should Hear How She Talks About You	Melissa Manchester
	4/03	3	5	37. Make A Move On Me	Olivia Newton-John
	9/04	2	5	38. Even The Nights Are Better	Air Supply
	3/20	2	5	39. Sweet Dreams	Air Supply
	7/17	2	5	40. Let It Whip	Dazz Band

1983 — Top 40 Hits

RANK	PK DATE	PK WKS	PK POS	TITLE	ARTIST
33	7/09	8	1	1. Every Breath You Take	The Police
53	3/05	7	1	2. Billie Jean	Michael Jackson
68	5/28	6	1	3. Flashdance...What A Feeling	Irene Cara
71	12/10	6	1	4. Say Say Say	Paul McCartney/ Michael Jackson
149	11/12	4	1	5. All Night Long (All Night)	Lionel Richie
161	10/01	4	1	6. Total Eclipse Of The Heart	Bonnie Tyler
167	1/15	4	1	7. Down Under	Men At Work
253	4/30	3	1	8. Beat It	Michael Jackson
378	10/29	2	1	9. Islands In The Stream	Kenny Rogers with Dolly Parton
407	2/19	2	1	10. Baby, Come To Me	Patti Austin with James Ingram
419	9/10	2	1	11. Maniac	Michael Sembello
642	5/21	1	1	12. Let's Dance	David Bowie
653	9/03	1	1	13. Sweet Dreams (Are Made of This)	Eurythmics
751	9/24	1	1	14. Tell Her About It	Billy Joel
827	2/05	1	1	15. Africa	Toto
837	4/23	1	1	16. Come On Eileen	Dexys Midnight Runners
955	7/02	5	2	17. Electric Avenue	Eddy Grant
973	12/17	4	2	18. Say It Isn't So	Daryl Hall-John Oates
979	2/26	4	2	19. Shame On The Moon	Bob Seger
	1/08	3	2	20. The Girl Is Mine	Michael Jackson/ Paul McCartney
	3/26	3	2	21. Do You Really Want To Hurt Me	Culture Club
	10/08	3	2	22. Making Love Out Of Nothing At All	Air Supply
	6/18	2	2	23. Time (Clock Of The Heart)	Culture Club
	5/07	1	2	24. Jeopardy	Greg Kihn Band
	11/12	5	3	25. Uptown Girl	Billy Joel
	9/10	4	3	26. The Safety Dance	Men Without Hats
	1/29	3	3	27. Sexual Healing	Marvin Gaye
	1/08	3	3	28. Dirty Laundry	Don Henley
	3/26	3	3	29. Hungry Like The Wolf	Duran Duran
	8/06	3	3	30. She Works Hard For The Money	Donna Summer
	12/24	3	3	31. Union Of The Snake	Duran Duran
	2/26	3	3	32. Stray Cat Strut	Stray Cats
	4/16	2	3	33. Mr. Roboto	Styx
	10/08	2	3	34. King Of Pain	The Police
	6/04	1	3	35. Overkill	Men At Work
	7/09	4	4	36. Never Gonna Let You Go	Sergio Mendes
	10/08	4	4	37. True	Spandau Ballet
	9/03	2	4	38. Puttin' On The Ritz	Taco
	3/26	2	4	39. You Are	Lionel Richie
	11/05	1	4	40. One Thing Leads To Another	The Fixx

RANK	PK DATE	PK WKS	PK POS	TITLE	ARTIST
86	12/22	6	1	1. Like A Virgin	Madonna
104	7/07	5	1	2. When Doves Cry	Prince
112	2/25	5	1	3. Jump	Van Halen
246	3/31	3	1	4. Footloose	Kenny Loggins
252	9/01	3	1	5. What's Love Got To Do With It	Tina Turner
257	4/21	3	1	6. Against All Odds (Take A Look At Me Now)	Phil Collins
260	10/13	3	1	7. I Just Called To Say I Love You	Stevie Wonder
263	8/11	3	1	8. Ghostbusters	Ray Parker Jr.
271	2/04	3	1	9. Karma Chameleon	Culture Club
289	11/17	3	1	10. Wake Me Up Before You Go-Go	Wham!
394	5/12	2	1	11. Hello	Lionel Richie
395	1/21	2	1	12. Owner Of A Lonely Heart	Yes
418	12/08	2	1	13. Out Of Touch	Daryl Hall John Oates
423	6/09	2	1	14. Time After Time	Cyndi Lauper
424	5/26	2	1	15. Let's Hear It For The Boy	Deniece Williams
425	9/29	2	1	16. Let's Go Crazy	Prince & the Revolution
463	6/23	2	1	17. The Reflex	Duran Duran
500	11/03	2	1	18. Caribbean Queen (No More Love On The Run)	Billy Ocean
658	9/22	1	1	19. Missing You	John Waite
975	6/30	4	2	20. Dancing In The Dark	Bruce Springsteen
980	12/15	4	2	21. The Wild Boys	Duran Duran
	3/24	3	2	22. Somebody's Watching Me	Rockwell
	3/10	2	2	23. Girls Just Want To Have Fun	Cyndi Lauper
	11/17	2	2	24. Purple Rain	Prince & the Revolution
	2/11	1	2	25. Joanna	Kool & The Gang
	3/03	1	2	26. 99 Luftballons	Nena
	11/24	3	3	27. I Feel For You	Chaka Khan
	9/08	3	3	28. She Bop	Cyndi Lauper
	1/28	3	3	29. Talking In Your Sleep	The Romantics
	9/29	3	3	30. Drive	The Cars
	8/04	3	3	31. State Of Shock	Jacksons
	7/07	2	3	32. Jump (For My Love)	Pointer Sisters
	5/05	2	3	33. Hold Me Now	Thompson Twins
	8/25	2	3	34. Stuck On You	Lionel Richie
	10/20	2	3	35. Hard Habit To Break	Chicago
	6/09	1	3	36. Oh Sherrie	Steve Perry
	3/31	2	4	37. Here Comes The Rain Again	Eurythmics
	6/30	2	4	38. Self Control	Laura Branigan
	7/14	2	4	39. Eyes Without A Face	Billy Idol
	3/03	*2	4	40. Thriller	Michael Jackson

1985   Top 40 Hits

RANK	PK DATE	PK WKS	PK POS	TITLE	ARTIST
185	12/21	4	1	1. Say You, Say Me	Lionel Richie
209	4/13	4	1	2. We Are The World	USA for Africa
270	2/16	3	1	3. Careless Whisper	Wham!
292	3/09	3	1	4. Can't Fight This Feeling	REO Speedwagon
299	9/21	3	1	5. Money For Nothing	Dire Straits
330	8/03	3	1	6. Shout	Tears For Fears
422	12/07	2	1	7. Broken Wings	Mr. Mister
456	2/02	2	1	8. I Want To Know What Love Is	Foreigner
464	8/24	2	1	9. The Power Of Love	Huey Lewis & The News
468	6/08	2	1	10. Everybody Wants To Rule The World	Tears For Fears
501	11/16	2	1	11. We Built This City	Starship
510	9/07	2	1	12. St. Elmo's Fire (Man In Motion)	John Parr
558	5/25	2	1	13. Everything She Wants	Wham!
560	6/22	2	1	14. Heaven	Bryan Adams
571	7/13	2	1	15. A View To A Kill	Duran Duran
576	3/30	2	1	16. One More Night	Phil Collins
661	11/30	1	1	17. Separate Lives	Phil Collins & Marilyn Martin
675	5/11	1	1	18. Crazy For You	Madonna
697	7/27	1	1	19. Everytime You Go Away	Paul Young
709	5/18	1	1	20. Don't You (Forget About Me)	Simple Minds
712	11/02	1	1	21. Part-Time Lover	Stevie Wonder
740	10/19	1	1	22. Take On Me	A-Ha
745	10/26	1	1	23. Saving All My Love For You	Whitney Houston
773	11/09	1	1	24. Miami Vice Theme	Jan Hammer
853	7/06	1	1	25. Sussudio	Phil Collins
856	10/12	1	1	26. Oh Sheila	Ready For The World
	12/28	3	2	27. Party All The Time	Eddie Murphy
	9/21	3	2	28. Cherish	Kool & The Gang
	2/02	2	2	29. Easy Lover	Philip Bailey (with Phil Collins)
	11/16	2	2	30. You Belong To The City	Glenn Frey
	1/12	2	2	31. All I Need	Jack Wagner
	3/23	2	2	32. Material Girl	Madonna
	2/23	1	2	33. Loverboy	Billy Ocean
	7/20	1	2	34. Raspberry Beret	Prince & the Revolution
	3/16	1	2	35. The Heat Is On	Glenn Frey
	9/14	1	2	36. We Don't Need Another Hero (Thunderdome)	Tina Turner
	6/01	3	3	37. Axel F	Harold Faltermeyer
	4/27	2	3	38. Rhythm Of The Night	DeBarge
	12/28	2	3	39. Alive & Kicking	Simple Minds
	1/19	2	3	40. You're The Inspiration	Chicago

Top 40 Hits   1986

RANK	PK DATE	PK WKS	PK POS	TITLE	ARTIST
168	1/18	4	1	1. That's What Friends Are For	Dionne & Friends
203	12/20	4	1	2. Walk Like An Egyptian	Bangles
323	6/14	3	1	3. On My Own	Patti LaBelle & Michael McDonald
327	5/17	3	1	4. Greatest Love Of All	Whitney Houston
331	9/20	3	1	5. Stuck With You	Huey Lewis & the News
333	3/29	3	1	6. Rock Me Amadeus	Falco
516	3/01	2	1	7. Kyrie	Mr. Mister
517	4/19	2	1	8. Kiss	Prince & The Revolution
518	8/16	2	1	9. Papa Don't Preach	Madonna
545	2/15	2	1	10. How Will I Know	Whitney Houston
554	8/02	2	1	11. Glory Of Love	Peter Cetera
568	10/11	2	1	12. When I Think Of You	Janet Jackson
575	10/25	2	1	13. True Colors	Cyndi Lauper
577	11/08	2	1	14. Amanda	Boston
699	12/13	1	1	15. The Way It Is	Bruce Hornsby & The Range
749	11/22	1	1	16. Human	Human League
755	5/03	1	1	17. Addicted To Love	Robert Palmer
758	7/05	1	1	18. There'll Be Sad Songs (To Make You Cry)	Billy Ocean
759	7/26	1	1	19. Sledgehammer	Peter Gabriel
760	5/10	1	1	20. West End Girls	Pet Shop Boys
774	9/13	1	1	21. Take My Breath Away	Berlin
777	3/15	1	1	22. Sara	Starship
791	9/06	1	1	23. Venus	Bananarama
834	12/06	1	1	24. The Next Time I Fall	Peter Cetera w/Amy Grant
836	11/29	1	1	25. You Give Love A Bad Name	Bon Jovi
838	7/12	1	1	26. Holding Back The Years	Simply Red
839	8/30	1	1	27. Higher Love	Steve Winwood
858	3/22	1	1	28. These Dreams	Heart
861	6/07	1	1	29. Live To Tell	Madonna
877	7/19	1	1	30. Invisible Touch	Genesis
	10/18	3	2	31. Typical Male	Tina Turner
	9/13	2	2	32. Dancing On The Ceiling	Lionel Richie
	12/27	2	2	33. Everybody Have Fun Tonight	Wang Chung
	9/27	2	2	34. Friends And Lovers	Gloria Loring & Carl Anderson
	2/01	2	2	35. Burning Heart	Survivor
	7/26	1	2	36. Danger Zone	Kenny Loggins
	10/11	1	2	37. Don't Forget Me (When I'm Gone)	Glass Tiger
	2/15	1	2	38. When The Going Gets Tough, The Tough Get Going	Billy Ocean
	4/19	1	2	39. Manic Monday	Bangles
	11/08	1	2	40. I Didn't Mean To Turn You On	Robert Palmer

RANK	PK DATE	PK WKS	PK POS	TITLE	ARTIST
187	12/12	4	1	1. Faith	George Michael
215	2/14	4	1	2. Livin' On A Prayer	Bon Jovi
288	7/11	3	1	3. Alone	Heart
300	5/16	3	1	4. With Or Without You	U2
325	8/29	3	1	5. La Bamba	Los Lobos
426	6/27	2	1	6. I Wanna Dance With Somebody (Who Loves Me)	Whitney Houston
462	4/04	2	1	7. Nothing's Gonna Stop Us Now	Starship
520	8/08	2	1	8. I Still Haven't Found What I'm Looking For	U2
522	9/26	2	1	9. Didn't We Almost Have It All	Whitney Houston
525	4/18	2	1	10. I Knew You Were Waiting (For Me)	Aretha Franklin & George Michael
547	1/24	2	1	11. At This Moment	Billy Vera & The Beaters
565	11/07	2	1	12. I Think We're Alone Now	Tiffany
569	5/02	2	1	13. (I Just) Died In Your Arms	Cutting Crew
579	3/21	2	1	14. Lean On Me	Club Nouveau
595	10/24	2	1	15. Bad	Michael Jackson
693	1/17	1	1	16. Shake You Down	Gregory Abbott
752	10/10	1	1	17. Here I Go Again	Whitesnake
756	6/13	1	1	18. Always	Atlantic Starr
762	6/20	1	1	19. Head To Toe	Lisa Lisa & Cult Jam
766	8/01	1	1	20. Shakedown	Bob Seger
832	12/05	1	1	21. Heaven Is A Place On Earth	Belinda Carlisle
833	11/28	1	1	22. (I've Had) The Time Of My Life	Bill Medley & Jennifer Warnes
851	2/07	1	1	23. Open Your Heart	Madonna
857	6/06	1	1	24. You Keep Me Hangin' On	Kim Wilde
859	10/17	1	1	25. Lost In Emotion	Lisa Lisa & Cult Jam
872	11/21	1	1	26. Mony Mony "Live"	Billy Idol
884	3/14	1	1	27. Jacob's Ladder	Huey Lewis & the News
888	8/22	1	1	28. Who's That Girl	Madonna
890	9/19	1	1	29. I Just Can't Stop Loving You	Michael Jackson
985	5/02	4	2	30. Looking For A New Love	Jody Watley
	10/24	3	2	31. Causing A Commotion	Madonna
	1/17	2	2	32. C'est La Vie	Robbie Nevil
	4/25	1	2	33. Don't Dream It's Over	Crowded House
	12/19	1	2	34. Is This Love	Whitesnake
	8/08	1	2	35. I Want Your Sex	George Michael
	10/17	1	2	36. U Got The Look	Prince
	1/10	1	2	37. Notorious	Duran Duran
	2/21	1	2	38. Keep Your Hands To Yourself	Georgia Satellites
	3/14	1	2	39. Somewhere Out There	Linda Ronstadt & James Ingram
	3/21	1	2	40. Let's Wait Awhile	Janet Jackson

Top 40 Hits   1988

RANK	PK DATE	PK WKS	PK POS	TITLE	ARTIST
214	7/30	4	1	1. Roll With It	Steve Winwood
290	12/24	3	1	2. Every Rose Has Its Thorn	Poison
328	5/28	3	1	3. One More Try	George Michael
454	12/10	2	1	4. Look Away	Chicago
507	3/12	2	1	5. Never Gonna Give You Up	Rick Astley
508	9/10	2	1	6. Sweet Child O' Mine	Guns N' Roses
509	5/14	2	1	7. Anything For You	Gloria Estefan
513	4/09	2	1	8. Get Outta My Dreams, Get Into My Car	Billy Ocean
521	3/26	2	1	9. Man In The Mirror	Michael Jackson
550	7/09	2	1	10. The Flame	Cheap Trick
557	2/06	2	1	11. Could've Been	Tiffany
563	9/24	2	1	12. Don't Worry Be Happy	Bobby McFerrin
564	10/22	2	1	13. Groovy Kind Of Love	Phil Collins
570	4/23	2	1	14. Where Do Broken Hearts Go	Whitney Houston
572	2/27	2	1	15. Father Figure	George Michael
574	11/19	2	1	16. Bad Medicine	Bon Jovi
581	8/27	2	1	17. Monkey	George Michael
690	1/30	1	1	18. Need You Tonight	INXS
700	1/16	1	1	19. Got My Mind Set On You	George Harrison
717	1/09	1	1	20. So Emotional	Whitney Houston
736	11/12	1	1	21. Wild, Wild West	The Escape Club
825	2/20	1	1	22. Seasons Change	Exposé
828	5/07	1	1	23. Wishing Well	Terence Trent D'Arby
829	12/03	1	1	24. Baby, I Love Your Way/ Freebird Medley (Free Baby)	Will To Power
830	7/23	1	1	25. Hold On To The Nights	Richard Marx
842	6/25	1	1	26. Foolish Beat	Debbie Gibson
846	10/08	1	1	27. Love Bites	Def Leppard
854	1/23	1	1	28. The Way You Make Me Feel	Michael Jackson
862	10/15	1	1	29. Red Red Wine	UB40
875	6/18	1	1	30. Together Forever	Rick Astley
899	11/05	1	1	31. Kokomo	The Beach Boys
915	7/02	1	1	32. Dirty Diana	Michael Jackson
	5/14	3	2	33. Shattered Dreams	Johnny Hates Jazz
	8/06	2	2	34. Hands To Heaven	Breathe
	3/26	2	2	35. Endless Summer Nights	Richard Marx
	9/10	2	2	36. Simply Irresistible	Robert Palmer
	2/20	2	2	37. What Have I Done To Deserve This?	Pet Shop Boys (and Dusty Springfield)
	4/16	2	2	38. Devil Inside	INXS
	7/09	2	2	39. Mercedes Boy	Pebbles
	7/23	1	2	40. Pour Some Sugar On Me	Def Leppard

RANK	PK DATE	PK WKS	PK POS	TITLE	ARTIST
175	12/23	4	1	1. Another Day In Paradise	Phil Collins
206	10/07	4	1	2. Miss You Much	Janet Jackson
320	2/11	3	1	3. Straight Up	Paula Abdul
329	8/12	3	1	4. Right Here Waiting	Richard Marx
334	3/04	3	1	5. Lost In Your Eyes	Debbie Gibson
335	4/22	3	1	6. Like A Prayer	Madonna
465	12/09	2	1	7. We Didn't Start The Fire	Billy Joel
519	1/21	2	1	8. Two Hearts	Phil Collins
548	11/11	2	1	9. When I See You Smile	Bad English
551	11/25	2	1	10. Blame It On The Rain	Milli Vanilli
552	5/20	2	1	11. Forever Your Girl	Paula Abdul
553	9/23	2	1	12. Girl I'm Gonna Miss You	Milli Vanilli
566	7/22	2	1	13. Toy Soldiers	Martika
701	9/02	1	1	14. Cold Hearted	Paula Abdul
721	9/16	1	1	15. Don't Wanna Lose You	Gloria Estefan
739	6/10	1	1	16. Wind Beneath My Wings	Bette Midler
742	1/14	1	1	17. My Prerogative	Bobby Brown
754	4/15	1	1	18. She Drives Me Crazy	Fine Young Cannibals
779	4/08	1	1	19. The Look	Roxette
831	7/15	1	1	20. If You Don't Know Me By Now	Simply Red
840	11/04	1	1	21. Listen To Your Heart	Roxette
841	6/17	1	1	22. I'll Be Loving You (Forever)	New Kids On The Block
843	7/01	1	1	23. Baby Don't Forget My Number	Milli Vanilli
845	3/25	1	1	24. The Living Years	Mike & The Mechanics
850	4/01	1	1	25. Eternal Flame	Bangles
855	5/13	1	1	26. I'll Be There For You	Bon Jovi
865	7/08	1	1	27. Good Thing	Fine Young Cannibals
879	9/09	1	1	28. Hangin' Tough	New Kids On The Block
886	8/05	1	1	29. Batdance	Prince
904	2/04	1	1	30. When I'm With You	Sheriff
905	6/03	1	1	31. Rock On	Michael Damian
910	6/24	1	1	32. Satisfied	Richard Marx
	8/05	3	2	33. On Our Own	Bobby Brown
	12/23	2	2	34. Don't Know Much	Linda Ronstadt (featuring Aaron Neville)
	9/23	2	2	35. Heaven	Warrant
	5/20	2	2	36. Real Love	Jody Watley
	10/07	2	2	37. Cherish	Madonna
	7/15	2	2	38. Express Yourself	Madonna
	4/01	1	2	39. Girl You Know It's True	Milli Vanilli
	1/21	1	2	40. Don't Rush Me	Taylor Dayne

Top 40 Hits 1990

RANK	PK DATE	PK WKS	PK POS	TITLE	ARTIST
170	12/08	4	1	1. Because I Love You (The Postman Song)	Stevie B
172	4/21	4	1	2. Nothing Compares 2 U	Sinéad O'Connor
213	8/04	4	1	3. Vision Of Love	Mariah Carey
286	5/19	3	1	4. Vogue	Madonna
293	3/03	3	1	5. Escapade	Janet Jackson
319	11/10	3	1	6. Love Takes Time	Mariah Carey
324	2/10	3	1	7. Opposites Attract	Paula Abdul with The Wild Pair
341	6/30	3	1	8. Step By Step	New Kids On The Block
349	1/20	3	1	9. How Am I Supposed To Live Without You	Michael Bolton
413	6/16	2	1	10. It Must Have Been Love	Roxette
502	3/24	2	1	11. Black Velvet	Alannah Myles
504	9/15	2	1	12. Release Me	Wilson Phillips
515	7/21	2	1	13. She Ain't Worth It	Glenn Medeiros/Bobby Brown
651	6/09	1	1	14. Hold On	Wilson Phillips
713	9/08	1	1	15. Blaze Of Glory	Jon Bon Jovi
716	12/01	1	1	16. I'm Your Baby Tonight	Whitney Houston
734	10/06	1	1	17. Close To You	Maxi Priest
741	10/20	1	1	18. I Don't Have The Heart	James Ingram
746	11/03	1	1	19. Ice Ice Baby	Vanilla Ice
753	9/29	1	1	20. (Can't Live Without Your) Love And Affection	Nelson
776	9/01	1	1	21. If Wishes Came True	Sweet Sensation
835	4/07	1	1	22. Love Will Lead You Back	Taylor Dayne
893	10/13	1	1	23. Praying For Time	George Michael
908	4/14	1	1	24. I'll Be Your Everything	Tommy Page
914	10/27	1	1	25. Black Cat	Janet Jackson
	4/14	3	2	26. Don't Wanna Fall In Love	Jane Child
	1/20	2	2	27. Pump Up The Jam	Technotronic Feat. Felly
	5/26	2	2	28. All I Wanna Do Is Make Love To You	Heart
	2/10	2	2	29. Two To Make It Right	Seduction
	1/06	2	2	30. Rhythm Nation	Janet Jackson
	3/03	2	2	31. Dangerous	Roxette
	8/18	2	2	32. Come Back To Me	Janet Jackson
	11/10	2	2	33. Pray	M.C. Hammer
	12/15	1	2	34. From A Distance	Bette Midler
	8/04	1	2	35. Cradle Of Love	Billy Idol
	7/21	1	2	36. Hold On	En Vogue
	8/11	1	2	37. The Power	Snap!
	5/05	1	2	38. I Wanna Be Rich	Calloway
	11/24	1	2	39. More Than Words Can Say	Alias
	6/09	4	3	40. Poison	Bell Biv DeVoe

1991 Top 40 Hits

RANK	PK DATE	PK WKS	PK POS	TITLE	ARTIST
55	7/27	7	1	1. (Everything I Do) I Do It For You	Bryan Adams
56	12/07	7	1	2. Black Or White	Michael Jackson
122	6/15	5	1	3. Rush, Rush	Paula Abdul
318	10/12	3	1	4. Emotions	Mariah Carey
412	2/09	2	1	5. Gonna Make You Sweat (Everybody Dance Now)	C & C Music Factory
453	1/26	2	1	6. The First Time	Surface
475	5/25	2	1	7. I Don't Wanna Cry	Mariah Carey
479	1/05	2	1	8. Justify My Love	Madonna
498	4/27	2	1	9. Baby Baby	Amy Grant
499	11/09	2	1	10. Cream	Prince & The N.P.G.
503	2/23	2	1	11. All The Man That I Need	Whitney Houston
506	3/09	2	1	12. Someday	Mariah Carey
511	9/21	2	1	13. I Adore Mi Amor	Color Me Badd
514	3/30	2	1	14. Coming Out Of The Dark	Gloria Estefan
654	6/08	1	1	15. More Than Words	Extreme
655	5/18	1	1	16. I Like The Way (The Kissing Game)	Hi-Five
656	3/23	1	1	17. One More Try	Timmy -T-
659	7/20	1	1	18. Unbelievable	EMF
662	11/23	1	1	19. When A Man Loves A Woman	Michael Bolton
688	11/30	1	1	20. Set Adrift On Memory Bliss	PM Dawn
733	11/02	1	1	21. Romantic	Karyn White
744	1/19	1	1	22. Love Will Never Do (Without You)	Janet Jackson
748	10/05	1	1	23. Good Vibrations	Marky Mark & Funky Bunch
765	4/20	1	1	24. You're In Love	Wilson Phillips
847	5/11	1	1	25. Joyride	Roxette
848	4/13	1	1	26. I've Been Thinking About You	Londonbeat
909	9/14	1	1	27. The Promise Of A New Day	Paula Abdul
966	12/14	4	2	28. It's So Hard To Say Goodbye To Yesterday	Boyz II Men
971	6/08	4	2	29. I Wanna Sex You Up	Color Me Badd
	10/19	2	2	30. Do Anything	Natural Selection
	5/18	2	2	31. Touch Me (All Night Long)	Cathy Dennis
	8/03	2	2	32. P.A.S.S.I.O.N.	Rythm Syndicate
	7/27	1	2	33. Right Here, Right Now	Jesus Jones
	11/16	1	2	34. Can't Stop This Thing We Started	Bryan Adams
	8/17	1	2	35. Every Heartbeat	Amy Grant
	8/24	1	2	36. It Ain't Over 'Til It's Over	Lenny Kravitz
	8/31	1	2	37. Fading Like A Flower (Every Time You Leave)	Roxette
	9/07	3	3	38. Motownphilly	Boyz II Men
	1/12	2	3	39. High Enough	Damn Yankees
	4/13	1	3	40. Hold You Tight	Tara Kemp

Top 40 Hits   1992

RANK	PK DATE	PK WKS	PK POS	TITLE	ARTIST
5	11/28	14	1	1. I Will Always Love You	Whitney Houston
6	8/15	13	1	2. End of the Road	Boyz II Men
34	4/25	8	1	3. Jump	Kris Kross
92	7/04	5	1	4. Baby Got Back	Sir Mix-A-Lot
100	3/21	5	1	5. Save The Best For Last	Vanessa Williams
241	2/08	3	1	6. I'm Too Sexy	Right Said Fred
268	2/29	3	1	7. To Be With You	Mr. Big
399	11/14	2	1	8. How Do You Talk To An Angel	The Heights
472	6/20	2	1	9. I'll Be There	Mariah Carey
608	1/25	1	1	10. All 4 Love	Color Me Badd
695	2/01	1	1	11. Don't Let The Sun Go Down On Me	George Michael/Elton John
714	8/08	1	1	12. This Used To Be My Playground	Madonna
938	11/21	8	2	13. If I Ever Fall In Love	Shai
945	8/15	6	2	14. Baby-Baby-Baby	TLC
946	9/26	6	2	15. Sometimes Love Just Ain't Enough	Patty Smyth with Don Henley
963	3/28	4	2	16. Tears In Heaven	Eric Clapton
992	12/26	3	2	17. Rump Shaker	Wreckx-N-Effect
997	5/16	3	2	18. My Lovin' (You're Never Gonna Get It)	En Vogue
	2/01	3	2	19. I Love Your Smile	Shanice
	6/06	1	2	20. Under The Bridge	Red Hot Chili Peppers
	1/25	1	2	21. Can't Let Go	Mariah Carey
	5/09	1	2	22. Bohemian Rhapsody	Queen
	10/31	4	3	23. I'd Die Without You	PM Dawn
	3/07	4	3	24. Remember The Time	Michael Jackson
	9/12	3	3	25. Humpin' Around	Bobby Brown
	10/10	2	3	26. Jump Around	House Of Pain
	8/29	2	3	27. November Rain	Guns N' Roses
	4/11	1	3	28. Masterpiece	Atlantic Starr
	2/15	1	3	29. Diamonds And Pearls	Prince & The N.P.G.
	10/24	1	3	30. Erotica	Madonna
	7/18	3	4	31. Achy Breaky Heart	Billy Ray Cyrus
	5/23	2	4	32. Live And Learn	Joe Public
	7/11	1	4	33. If You Asked Me To	Celine Dion
	9/19	1	4	34. Stay	Shakespear's Sister
	1/18	2	5	35. Finally	Ce Ce Peniston
	6/27	2	5	36. Damn I Wish I Was Your Lover	Sophie B. Hawkins
	8/01	1	5	37. Just Another Day	Jon Secada
	10/17	1	5	38. She's Playing Hard To Get	Hi-Five
	4/11	1	5	39. Make It Happen	Mariah Carey
	1/11	1	5	40. 2 Legit 2 Quit	Hammer

RANK	PK DATE	PK WKS	PK POS	#	TITLE	ARTIST
31	9/11	8	1	1.	Dreamlover	Mariah Carey
32	5/15	8	1	2.	That's The Way Love Goes	Janet Jackson
41	7/24	7	1	3.	Can't Help Falling In Love	UB40
45	3/13	7	1	4.	Informer	Snow
98	11/06	5	1	5.	I'd Do Anything For Love (But I Won't Do That)	Meat Loaf
140	12/25	4	1	6.	Hero	Mariah Carey
360	5/01	2	1	7.	Freak Me	Silk
363	7/10	2	1	8.	Weak	SWV
364	12/11	2	1	9.	Again	Janet Jackson
633	3/06	1	1	10.	A Whole New World (Aladdin's Theme)	Peabo Bryson & Regina Belle
940	7/31	7	2	11.	Whoomp! (There It Is)	Tag Team
988	11/06	3	2	12.	All That She Wants	Ace Of Base
	10/02	3	2	13.	Right Here/Human Nature	SWV
	3/20	1	2	14.	Nuthin' But A "G" Thang	Dr. Dre
	10/23	1	2	15.	Just Kickin' It	Xscape
	5/22	7	3	16.	Knockin' Da Boots	H-Town
	1/16	3	3	17.	In The Still Of The Nite (I'll Remember)	Boyz II Men
	2/20	3	3	18.	Ordinary World	Duran Duran
	10/16	1	3	19.	The River Of Dreams	Billy Joel
	5/15	1	3	20.	Love Is	Vanessa Williams & Brian McKnight
	8/21	1	3	21.	I'm Gonna Be (500 Miles)	The Proclaimers
	4/03	5	4	22.	I Have Nothing	Whitney Houston
	9/11	2	4	23.	If	Janet Jackson
	11/20	2	4	24.	Gangsta Lean	D.R.S.
	1/30	2	4	25.	Saving Forever For You	Shanice
	8/28	2	4	26.	Lately	Jodeci
	2/20	2	4	27.	I'm Every Woman	Whitney Houston
	3/27	1	4	28.	Don't Walk Away	Jade
	12/04	1	4	29.	Shoop	Salt-N-Pepa
	8/21	1	4	30.	Slam	Onyx
	8/28	3	5	31.	Runaway Train	Soul Asylum
	6/19	3	5	32.	Have I Told You Lately	Rod Stewart
	1/02	1	5	33.	Rhythm Is A Dancer	Snap!
	6/12	1	5	34.	Show Me Love	Robin S
	5/22	2	6	35.	I'm So Into You	SWV
	2/20	2	6	36.	Mr. Wendal	Arrested Development
	5/29	2	6	37.	Looking Through Patient Eyes	PM Dawn
	10/30	2	6	38.	Hey Mr. D.J.	Zhané
	4/10	1	6	39.	Cats In The Cradle	Ugly Kid Joe
	8/07	3	7	40.	If I Had No Loot	Tony Toni Tone

Top 40 Hits   1994

RANK	PK DATE	PK WKS	PK POS	TITLE	ARTIST
3	8/27	14	1	1. I'll Make Love To You	Boyz II Men
11	5/21	11	1	2. I Swear	All-4-One
57	3/12	6	1	3. The Sign	Ace Of Base
59	12/03	6	1	4. On Bended Knee	Boyz II Men
138	2/12	4	1	5. The Power Of Love	Celine Dion
151	4/09	4	1	6. Bump N' Grind	R. Kelly
223	8/06	3	1	7. Stay (I Missed You)	Lisa Loeb & Nine Stories
228	1/22	3	1	8. All For Love	Bryan Adams/ Rod Stewart/Sting
362	12/17	2	1	9. Here Comes The Hotstepper	Ini Kamoze
944	10/08	6	2	10. All I Wanna Do	Sheryl Crow
969	5/28	4	2	11. I'll Remember	Madonna
	7/02	3	2	12. Regulate	Warren G. & Nate Dogg
	6/25	1	2	13. Any Time, Any Place	Janet Jackson
	10/01	1	2	14. Endless Love	Luther Vandross & Mariah Carey
	11/12	11	3	15. Another Night	Real McCoy
	3/19	6	3	16. Without You	Mariah Carey
	7/30	5	3	17. Fantastic Voyage	Coolio
	1/22	3	3	18. Breathe Again	Toni Braxton
	2/26	3	3	19. Whatta Man	Salt 'N' Pepa with En Vogue
	4/30	3	3	20. The Most Beautiful Girl In The World	Prince
	9/03	2	3	21. Wild Night	John Mellencamp/ Me'Shell Ndegéocello
	11/05	1	3	22. Secret	Madonna
	9/17	1	3	23. Stroke You Up	Changing Faces
	12/10	6	4	24. Always	Bon Jovi
	9/10	5	4	25. When Can I See You	Babyface
	6/18	4	4	26. Don't Turn Around	Ace Of Base
	4/16	2	4	27. Mmm Mmm Mmm Mmm	Crash Test Dummies
	5/07	2	4	28. Return To Innocence	Enigma
	8/06	1	4	29. Can You Feel The Love Tonight	Elton John
	3/12	3	5	30. So Much In Love	All-4-One
	7/02	1	5	31. Back & Forth	Aaliyah
	10/15	1	5	32. Never Lie	Immature
	5/14	4	6	33. Baby, I Love Your Way	Big Mountain
	12/31	3	6	34. I Wanna Be Down	Brandy
	1/22	2	6	35. Said I Loved You...But I Lied	Michael Bolton
	10/15	2	6	36. At Your Best (You Are Love)	Aaliyah
	8/13	1	6	37. Funkdafied	Da Brat
	5/28	4	7	38. You Mean The World To Me	Toni Braxton
	3/19	3	7	39. Now and Forever	Richard Marx
	2/12	1	7	40. Getto Jam	Domino

1995   Top 40 Hits

RANK	PK DATE	PK WKS	PK POS	TITLE	ARTIST
1	12/02	16	1	1. One Sweet Day	Mariah Carey & Boyz II Men
27	9/30	8	1	2. Fantasy	Mariah Carey
38	7/08	7	1	3. Waterfalls	TLC
40	2/25	7	1	4. Take A Bow	Madonna
43	4/15	7	1	5. This Is How We Do It	Montell Jordan
101	6/03	5	1	6. Have You Ever Really Loved A Woman?	Bryan Adams
132	1/28	4	1	7. Creep	TLC
220	9/09	3	1	8. Gangsta's Paradise	Coolio Feat. L.V.
603	8/26	1	1	9. Kiss From A Rose	Seal
605	11/25	1	1	10. Exhale (Shoop Shoop)	Whitney Houston
641	9/02	1	1	11. You Are Not Alone	Michael Jackson
964	3/18	4	2	12. Candy Rain	Soul For Real
995	7/01	3	2	13. Don't Take It Personal (just one of dem days)	Monica
	4/15	3	2	14. Red Light Special	TLC
	7/15	3	2	15. One More Chance/Stay With Me	The Notorious B.I.G.
	5/06	2	2	16. Freak Like Me	Adina Howard
	6/17	1	2	17. Water Runs Dry	Boyz II Men
	6/24	1	2	18. Total Eclipse Of The Heart	Nicki French
	12/02	8	3	19. Hey Lover	LL Cool J
	10/21	5	3	20. Runaway	Janet Jackson
	8/19	2	3	21. Boombastic	Shaggy
	4/08	1	3	22. Run Away	Real McCoy
	6/03	1	3	23. I'll Be There For You/You're All I Need To Get By	Method Man feat. Mary J. Blige
	5/06	2	4	24. I Know	Dionne Farris
	3/11	2	4	25. Baby	Brandy
	11/18	2	4	26. You Remind Me Of Something	R. Kelly
	8/26	1	4	27. Colors Of The Wind	Vanessa Williams
	3/25	3	5	28. Strong Enough	Sheryl Crow
	12/30	3	5	29. Diggin' On You	TLC
	11/04	3	5	30. Tell Me	Groove Theory
	6/17	2	5	31. Scream	Michael Jackson & Janet Jackson
	8/26	1	5	32. I Can Love You Like That	All-4-One
	3/11	1	5	33. You Gotta Be	Des'ree
	10/28	3	6	34. As I Lay Me Down	Sophie B. Hawkins
	3/18	2	6	35. Big Poppa	The Notorious B.I.G.
	10/21	1	6	36. Only Wanna Be With You	Hootie & The Blowfish
	12/16	1	6	37. You'll See	Madonna
	1/07	4	7	38. Before I Let You Go	BLACKstreet
	11/11	2	7	39. Back For Good	Take That
	12/30	1	7	40. Before You Walk Out Of My Life	Monica

Top 40 Hits   1996

RANK	PK DATE	PK WKS	PK POS	TITLE	ARTIST
2	8/03	14	1	1. Macarena (bayside boys mix)	Los Del Rio
9	12/07	11	1	2. Un-Break My Heart	Toni Braxton
36	5/18	8	1	3. Tha Crossroads	Bone thugs-n-harmony
58	3/23	6	1	4. Because You Loved Me	Celine Dion
133	11/09	4	1	5. No Diggity	BLACKstreet
361	5/04	2	1	6. Always Be My Baby	Mariah Carey
382	7/13	2	1	7. How Do U Want It	2 Pac (feat. KC & JoJo)
600	7/27	1	1	8. You're Makin' Me High	Toni Braxton
935	8/24	9	2	9. I Love You Always Forever	Donna Lewis
951	10/26	5	2	10. It's All Coming Back To Me Now	Celine Dion
959	12/21	4	2	11. I Believe I Can Fly	R. Kelly
	3/23	2	2	12. Nobody Knows	The Tony Rich Project
	3/09	2	2	13. Sittin' Up In My Room	Brandy feat. LL Cool J
	2/24	2	2	14. Not Gon' Cry	Mary J. Blige
	8/17	1	2	15. Twisted	Keith Sweat
	2/17	1	2	16. Missing	Everything But The Girl
	6/15	5	3	17. Give Me One Reason	Tracy Chapman
	12/07	2	3	18. Nobody	Keith Sweat
	8/17	1	3	19. C'Mon N' Ride It (The Train)	Quad City DJ's
	8/24	1	3	20. Loungin	LL Cool J
	8/31	1	3	21. Hit Me Off	New Edition
	4/13	5	4	22. Ironic	Alanis Morissette
	11/23	2	4	23. Mouth	Merril Bainbridge
	3/30	2	4	24. Down Low (Nobody Has To Know)	R. Kelly (feat. Ronald Isley & Ernie Isley)
	2/03	2	4	25. One Of Us	Joan Osborne
	10/12	3	5	26. Where Do You Go	No Mercy
	8/17	2	5	27. Change The World	Eric Clapton
	4/27	2	5	28. 1,2,3,4 (Sumpin' New)	Coolio
	1/27	1	5	29. Name	Goo Goo Dolls
	8/03	1	5	30. I Can't Sleep Baby (If I)	R. Kelly
	6/08	1	5	31. You're The One	SWV
	1/20	1	5	32. Breakfast At Tiffany's	Deep Blue Something
	2/24	3	6	33. Be My Lover	La Bouche
	11/23	2	6	34. Pony	Ginuwine
	6/22	1	6	35. California Love	2 Pac (feat. Dr. Dre & Roger Troutman)
	7/27	1	6	36. You Learn	Alanis Morissette
	11/09	1	6	37. This Is For The Lover In You	Babyface
	1/06	1	6	38. Free As A Bird	The Beatles
	6/22	2	7	39. Theme From Mission: Impossible	Adam Clayton & Larry Mullen
	2/24	2	7	40. Jesus To A Child	George Michael

1997

Top 40 Hits

RANK	PK DATE	PK WKS	PK POS		TITLE	ARTIST
4	10/11	14	1	1.	Candle In The Wind 1997/	Elton John
					Something About The Way You Look Tonight	Elton John
12	6/14	11	1	2.	I'll Be Missing You	Puff Daddy &
						Faith Evans (Feat. 112)
61	3/22	6	1	3.	Can't Nobody Hold Me Down	Puff Daddy Feat. Ma$e
143	2/22	4	1	4.	Wannabe	Spice Girls
237	5/24	3	1	5.	MMMBop	Hanson
284	9/13	3	1	6.	Honey	Mariah Carey
291	5/03	3	1	7.	Hypnotize	The Notorious B.I.G.
376	8/30	2	1	8.	Mo Money Mo Problems	The Notorious B.I.G. Feat.
						Puff Daddy & Ma$e
631	10/04	1	1	9.	4 Seasons Of Loneliness	Boyz II Men
941	10/25	7	2	10.	You Make Me Wanna…	Usher
956	12/13	4	2	11.	How Do I Live	LeAnn Rimes
958	1/18	4	2	12.	Don't Let Go (Love)	En Vogue
965	7/12	4	2	13.	Bitch	Meredith Brooks
	4/19	2	2	14.	You Were Meant For Me	Jewel
	9/06	2	2	15.	Quit Playing Games (With My Heart)	Backstreet Boys
	6/07	1	2	16.	Return Of The Mack	Mark Morrison
	5/31	3	3	17.	Say You'll Be There	Spice Girls
	8/09	4	4	18.	Semi-Charmed Life	Third Eye Blind
	4/19	4	4	19.	For You I Will	Monica
	12/06	3	4	20.	My Body	LSG
	4/05	2	4	21.	All By Myself	Celine Dion
	11/29	1	4	22.	My Love Is The Shhh!	Somethin' For The People
	3/29	1	4	23.	In My Bed	Dru Hill
	9/06	1	4	24.	2 Become 1	Spice Girls
	2/01	1	4	25.	I Believe In You And Me	Whitney Houston
	5/10	1	4	26.	I Want You	Savage Garden
	11/22	1	4	27.	All Cried Out	Allure
	6/21	1	4	28.	Look Into My Eyes	Bone Thugs-N-Harmony
	12/13	2	5	29.	Feel So Good	Mase
	6/07	1	5	30.	The Freshmen	The Verve Pipe
	11/29	3	6	31.	Tubthumping	Chumbawamba
	3/22	3	6	32.	Every Time I Close My Eyes	Babyface
	6/07	2	6	33.	I Belong To You (Every Time I See Your Face)	Rome
	8/09	1	6	34.	Not Tonight	Lil' Kim
	11/29	3	7	35.	Show Me Love	Robyn
	11/01	2	7	36.	Foolish Games	Jewel
	8/02	2	7	37.	Do You Know (What It Takes)	Robyn
	1/11	1	7	38.	I'm Still In Love With You	New Edition
	7/26	1	7	39.	Sunny Came Home	Shawn Colvin
	7/19	1	7	40.	It's Your Love	Tim McGraw & Faith Hill

Top 40 Hits   1998

RANK	PK DATE	PK WKS	PK POS	TITLE	ARTIST
7	6/06	13	1	1. The Boy Is Mine	Brandy & Monica
83	12/05	6	1	2. I'm Your Angel	R. Kelly & Celine Dion
88	4/25	5	1	3. Too Close	Next
90	10/03	5	1	4. The First Night	Monica
174	9/05	4	1	5. I Don't Want To Miss A Thing	Aerosmith
234	4/04	3	1	6. All My Life	K-Ci & JoJo
348	3/14	3	1	7. Gettin' Jiggy Wit It	Will Smith
357	1/17	2	1	8. Truly Madly Deeply	Savage Garden
366	1/31	2	1	9. Together Again	Janet
368	2/14	2	1	10. Nice & Slow	Usher
384	11/14	2	1	11. Doo Wop (That Thing)	Lauryn Hill
457	2/28	2	1	12. My Heart Will Go On (Love Theme From 'Titanic')	Celine Dion
609	11/28	1	1	13. Lately	Divine
620	5/23	1	1	14. My All	Mariah Carey
663	10/17	1	1	15. One Week	Barenaked Ladies
934	5/02	9	2	16. You're Still The One	Shania Twain
936	12/05	8	2	17. Nobody's Supposed To Be Here	Deborah Cox
989	8/15	3	2	18. My Way	Usher
	4/11	2	2	19. Let's Ride	Montell Jordan
	1/03	2	2	20. It's All About The Benjamins	Puff Daddy
	4/04	1	2	21. Frozen	Madonna
	9/05	4	3	22. Crush	Jennifer Paige
	10/24	3	3	23. How Deep Is Your Love	Dru Hill
	11/21	1	3	24. Because Of You	98°
	8/22	1	3	25. Adia	Sarah McLachlan
	3/28	1	3	26. No, No, No (Part 2)	Destiny's Child
	5/23	1	3	27. I Get Lonely	Janet Jackson
	5/09	2	4	28. Everybody (Backstreet's Back)	Backstreet Boys
	12/19	2	4	29. From This Moment On	Shania Twain
	7/25	1	4	30. Come With Me	Puff Daddy
	8/22	1	4	31. Never Ever	All Saints
	1/24	1	4	32. Been Around The World	Puff Daddy
	8/01	3	5	33. Make It Hot	Nicole
	10/03	2	5	34. I'll Be	Edwin McCain
	5/16	1	5	35. Body Bumpin' (Yippie Yi-Yo)	Public Announcement
	7/11	1	5	36. Ray Of Light	Madonna
	2/07	3	6	37. I Don't Ever Want To See You Again	Uncle Sam
	5/16	3	6	38. It's All About Me	Mya
	9/12	2	6	39. Daydreamin'	Tatyana Ali
	4/18	2	6	40. Romeo And Juliet	Sylk-E. Fyne

1999 Top 40 Hits

RANK	PK DATE	PK WKS	PK POS	TITLE	ARTIST
8	10/23	12	1	1. Smooth	Santana Feat. Rob Thomas
93	6/12	5	1	2. If You Had My Love	Jennifer Lopez
95	7/31	5	1	3. Genie In A Bottle	Christina Aguilera
99	5/08	5	1	4. Livin' La Vida Loca	Ricky Martin
136	4/10	4	1	5. No Scrubs	TLC
139	3/13	4	1	6. Believe	Cher
142	2/13	4	1	7. Angel Of Mine	Monica
227	9/18	3	1	8. Unpretty	TLC
367	1/30	2	1	9. …Baby One More Time	Britney Spears
372	1/16	2	1	10. Have You Ever?	Brandy
470	10/09	2	1	11. Heartbreaker	Mariah Carey (Feat. Jay-Z)
546	9/04	2	1	12. Bailamos	Enrique Iglesias
637	7/17	1	1	13. Bills, Bills, Bills	Destiny's Child
852	7/24	1	1	14. Wild Wild West	Will Smith Feat. Dru Hill & Kool Mo Dee
937	11/20	8	2	15. Back At One	Brian McKnight
994	3/20	3	2	16. Heartbreak Hotel	Whitney Houston (Feat. Faith Evans & Kelly Price)
	10/30	3	2	17. Satisfy You	Puff Daddy
	9/25	2	2	18. She's All I Ever Had	Ricky Martin
	5/01	1	2	19. Kiss Me	Sixpence None The Richer
	6/26	1	2	20. Last Kiss	Pearl Jam
	8/14	1	2	21. Tell Me It's Real	K-Ci & JoJo
	10/16	1	2	22. Music Of My Heart	*NSYNC & Gloria Estefan
	12/11	5	3	23. I Wanna Love You Forever	Jessica Simpson
	8/28	4	3	24. Summer Girls	LFO
	4/03	3	3	25. Every Morning	Sugar Ray
	11/27	2	3	26. I Need To Know	Marc Anthony
	11/13	2	3	27. Mambo No. 5 (A Little Bit Of…)	Lou Bega
	4/17	1	3	28. What's It Gonna Be?!	Busta Rhymes
	5/29	3	4	29. Fortunate	Maxwell
	3/06	2	4	30. Angel	Sarah McLachlan
	3/20	2	4	31. I Still Believe	Mariah Carey
	6/19	1	4	32. Where My Girls At?	702
	8/14	1	4	33. All Star	Smash Mouth
	7/03	1	4	34. It's Not Right But It's Okay	Whitney Houston
	2/06	2	5	35. All I Have To Give	Backstreet Boys
	5/22	1	5	36. Who Dat	JT Money
	1/23	1	5	37. Save Tonight	Eagle-Eye Cherry
	7/03	1	5	38. The Hardest Thing	98°
	1/30	1	5	39. Jumper	Third Eye Blind
	9/11	1	5	40. Lost In You	Garth Brooks as Chris Gaines

RANK	PK DATE	PK WKS	PK POS	TITLE	ARTIST
13	11/18	11	1	1. Independent Women Part 1	Destiny's Child
15	4/08	10	1	2. Maria Maria	Santana Feat. The Product G&B
135	1/29	4	1	3. I Knew I Loved You	Savage Garden
152	9/16	4	1	4. Music	Madonna
202	10/14	4	1	5. Come On Over Baby (all I want is you)	Christina Aguilera
236	8/26	3	1	6. Doesn't Really Matter	Janet
242	3/18	3	1	7. Say My Name	Destiny's Child
255	6/24	3	1	8. Be With You	Enrique Iglesias
373	8/12	2	1	9. Incomplete	Sisqó
375	3/04	2	1	10. Amazed	Lonestar
381	7/29	2	1	11. It's Gonna Be Me	*NSYNC
497	1/15	2	1	12. What A Girl Wants	Christina Aguilera
601	7/15	1	1	13. Everything You Want	Vertical Horizon
602	11/11	1	1	14. With Arms Wide Open	Creed
604	6/17	1	1	15. Try Again	Aaliyah
607	7/22	1	1	16. Bent	Matchbox Twenty
929	2/19	1	1	17. Thank God I Found You	Mariah With Joe & 98°
950	4/22	5	2	18. Breathe	Faith Hill
998	12/02	3	2	19. Case Of The Ex (Whatcha Gonna Do)	Mya
	5/06	2	2	20. He Wasn't Man Enough	Toni Braxton
	6/03	2	2	21. You Sang To Me	Marc Anthony
	9/30	2	2	22. Give Me Just One Night (Una Noche)	98°
	8/19	5	3	23. Jumpin', Jumpin'	Destiny's Child
	11/11	3	3	24. Kryptonite	3 Doors Down
	5/20	3	3	25. Thong Song	Sisqó
	7/01	2	3	26. I Turn To You	Christina Aguilera
	1/01	2	4	27. My Love Is Your Love	Whitney Houston
	7/01	2	4	28. I Wanna Know	Joe
	2/12	2	4	29. Get It On...Tonite	Montell Jordan
	4/15	2	4	30. Bye Bye Bye	*NSYNC
	6/24	2	4	31. The Real Slim Shady	Eminem
	11/25	1	4	32. Most Girls	Pink
	12/09	1	4	33. Gotta Tell You	Samantha Mumba
	1/22	2	5	34. Bring It All To Me	Blaque
	1/08	1	5	35. Hot Boyz	Missy "Misdemeanor" Elliott [feat. Nas, Eve & Q-Tip]
	5/20	1	5	36. I Try	Macy Gray
	12/02	1	5	37. This I Promise You	*NSYNC
	9/02	1	5	38. No More	Ruff Endz
	3/18	3	6	39. Show Me The Meaning Of Being Lonely	Backstreet Boys
	7/22	2	6	40. Absolutely story of a girl	Ninedays

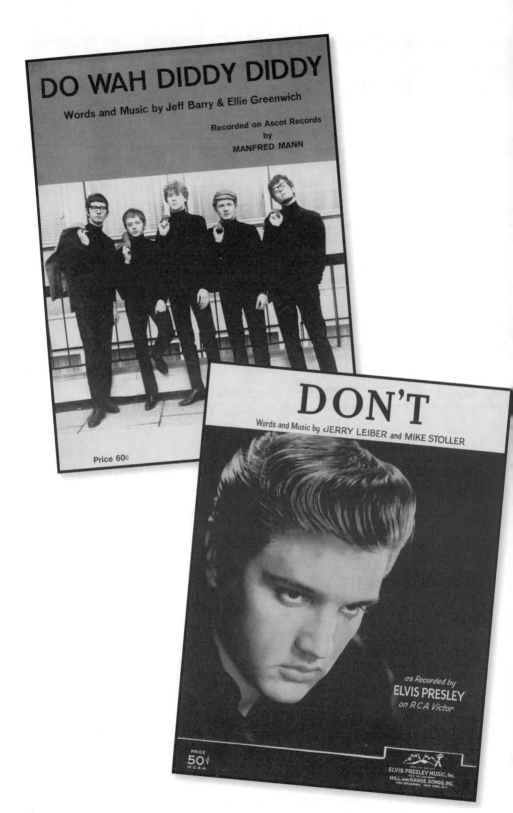

THE TOP 100 ALBUMS

This section displays, in rank order, the biggest #1 albums of *Billboard* magazine's pop albums charts from January 1, 1955 through December 30, 2000.

This ranking is based on the most weeks an album held the #1 position. Ties are broken accordly: total weeks in the Top 10, total weeks in the Top 40, total weeks charted.

The total weeks at #1 and total weeks in the Top 10 are shown beside each album cover photo, along with the year the album peaked.

1.
"West Side Story"
Soundtrack

#1 – 54 Weeks
Top 10 Weeks: 106
Year: 1962

3.
"South Pacific"
Soundtrack

#1 – 31 Weeks
Top 10 Weeks: 90
Year: 1958

5.
"Rumours"
Fleetwood Mac

#1 – 31 Weeks
Top 10 Weeks: 52
Year: 1977

7.
"Purple Rain"
Prince And The Revolution/ Soundtrack

#1 – 24 Weeks
Top 10 Weeks: 32
Year: 1984

9.
"The Bodyguard"
**Whitney Houston/
Soundtrack**

#1 – 20 Weeks
Top 10 Weeks: 40
Year: 1992

11.
"Ropin' The Wind"
Garth Brooks

#1 – 18 Weeks
Top 10 Weeks: 50
Year: 1991

13.
"More Of The
Monkees"
The Monkees

#1 – 18 Weeks
Top 10 Weeks: 25
Year: 1967

15.
"Synchronicity"
The Police

#1 – 17 Weeks
Top 10 Weeks: 40
Year: 1983

17.
"The Sound Of Music"
Original Cast

#1 – 16 Weeks
Top 10 Weeks: 105
Year: 1960

18.
"To The Extreme"
Vanilla Ice

#1 – 16 Weeks
Top 10 Weeks: 2
Year: 1990

19.
"Days of Wine And Roses"
Andy Williams

#1 – 16 Weeks
Top 10 Weeks: 23
Year: 1963

20.
"Titanic"
Soundtrack

#1 – 16 Weeks
Top 10 Weeks: 2
Year: 1998

21.
"My Fair Lady"
Original Cast

#1 – 15 Weeks
Top 10 Weeks: 173
Year: 1956

22.
"Tapestry"
Carole King

#1 – 15 Weeks
Top 10 Weeks: 4
Year: 1971

23.
"Sgt. Pepper's Lonely Hearts Club Band"
The Beatles

#1 – 15 Weeks
Top 10 Weeks: 33
Year: 1967

24.
"Business As Usual"
Men At Work

#1 – 15 Weeks
Top 10 Weeks: 31
Year: 1982

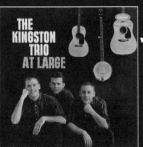

25.
"The Kingston Trio At Large"
The Kingston Trio

#1 – 15 Weeks
Top 10 Weeks: 31
Year: 1959

26.
"Hi Infidelity"
REO Speedwagon

#1 – 15 Weeks
Top 10 Weeks: 30
Year: 1981

27.
"The Wall"
Pink Floyd

#1 – 15 Weeks
Top 10 Weeks: 27
Year: 1980

28.
"Mary Poppins"
Soundtrack

#1 – 14 Weeks
Top 10 Weeks: 48
Year: 1965

29.
"Whitney Houston"
Whitney Houston

#1 – 14 Weeks
Top 10 Weeks: 46
Year: 1986

30.
"The Button Down Mind Of Bob Newha
Bob Newhart

#1 – 14 Weeks
Top 10 Weeks: 4
Year: 1960

31.
"Exodus"
Soundtrack

#1 – 14 Weeks
Top 10 Weeks: 38
Year: 1961

32.
"Songs In Th Key Of Life"
Stevie Wonder

#1 –14 Weeks
Top 10 Weeks: 35
Year: 1976

33.
"Modern Sounds In Country And Western Music"
Ray Charles

#1 – 14 Weeks
Top 10 Weeks: 33
Year: 1962

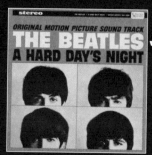

34.
"A Hard Day's Night"
The Beatles/ Soundtrack

#1 – 14 Weeks
Top 10 Weeks: 28
Year: 1964

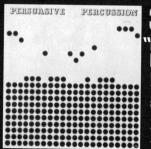

35.
"Persuasive Percussion"
Enoch Light/ Terry Snyder and The All-Stars

#1 – 13 Weeks
Top 10 Weeks: 43
Year: 1960

36.
"Judy At Carnegie Hal
Judy Garland

#1 – 13 Weeks
Top 10 Weeks: 37
Year: 1961

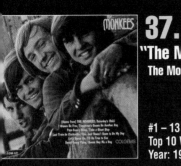

37.
"The Monkees"
The Monkees

#1 – 13 Weeks
Top 10 Weeks: 32
Year: 1966

39.
"Jagged Little Pill"
Alanis Morissette

#1 – 12 Weeks
Top 10 Weeks: 69
Year: 1995

41.
"Faith"
George Michael

#1 – 12 Weeks
Top 10 Weeks: 51
Year: 1988

43.
"Supernatural"
Santana

#1 – 12 Weeks
Top 10 Weeks: 44
Year: 1999

45.
"Grease"
Soundtrack

#1 – 12 Weeks
Top 10 Weeks: 29
Year: 1978

46.
"The First Family"
Vaughn Meader

#1 – 12 Weeks
Top 10 Weeks: 17
Year: 1962

47.
"Mariah Carey"
Mariah Carey

#1 – 11 Weeks
Top 10 Weeks: 49
Year: 1991

48.
"Calcutta!"
Lawrence Welk

#1 – 11 Weeks
Top 10 Weeks: 33
Year: 1961

49.
"Whitney"
Whitney Houston

#1 – 11 Weeks
Top 10 Weeks: 31
Year: 1987

50.
"Abbey Road"
The Beatles

#1 – 11 Weeks
Top 10 Weeks: 27
Year: 1969

51.
"Meet The Beatles!"
The Beatles

#1 – 11 Weeks
Top 10 Weeks: 21
Year: 1964

52.
"Miami Vice"
TV Soundtrack

#1 – 11 Weeks
Top 10 Weeks: 18
Year: 1985

53.
"Forever Your Girl"
Paula Abdul

#1 –10 Weeks
Top 10 Weeks: 64
Year: 1989

54.
"Around The World In 80 Days"
Soundtrack

#1 – 10 Weeks
Top 10 Weeks: 54
Year: 1957

55.
"Gigi"
Soundtrack

#1 – 10 Weeks
Top 10 Weeks: 54
Year: 1958

56.
"Frampton Comes Alive!"
Peter Frampton

#1 – 10 Weeks
Top 10 Weeks: 52
Year: 1976

57.
"Elvis Presley"
Elvis Presley

#1 – 10 Weeks
Top 10 Weeks: 43
Year: 1956

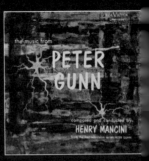

59.
"Millennium"
Backstreet Boys

#1 – 10 Weeks
Top 10 Weeks: 37
Year: 1999

61.
"The Lion King"
Soundtrack

#1 – 10 Weeks
Top 10 Weeks: 31
Year: 1994

63.
"Footloose"
Soundtrack

#1 – 10 Weeks
Top 10 Weeks: 20
Year: 1984

65.
"Loving You"
**Elvis Presley/
Soundtrack**

#1 – 10 Weeks
Top 10 Weeks: 19
Year: 1957

67.
"Bridge Over Troubled Water"
Simon and Garfunkel

#1 – 10 Weeks
Top 10 Weeks: 17
Year: 1970

69.
"Brothers In Arms"
Dire Straits

#1 – 9 Weeks
Top 10 Weeks: 37
Year: 1985

71.
"The Joshua Tree"
U2

#1 – 9 Weeks
Top 10 Weeks: 35
Year: 1987

73.
"Asia"
Asia

#1 – 9 Weeks
Top 10 Weeks: 27
Year: 1982

74.
"The Graduate
Simon & Garfunke
Soundtrack

#1 – 9 Weeks
Top 10 Weeks: 26
Year: 1968

75.
"American Fool"
John Cougar

#1 – 9 Weeks
Top 10 Weeks: 22
Year: 1982

76.
"Tatoo You"
The Rolling Stone

#1 – 9 Weeks
Top 10 Weeks: 22
Year: 1981

77.
**"Stars For A
Summer Night"**
Various Artists

#1 – 9 Weeks
Top 10 Weeks: 21
Year: 1961

78.
"The Long Ru
Eagles

#1 – 9 Weeks
Top 10 Weeks: 21
Year: 1979

79.
"Nice 'n' Easy"
Frank Sinatra

#1 – 9 Weeks
Top 10 Weeks: 19
Year: 1960

80.
"Cosmo's Factory"
Creedence Clearwater Revival

#1 – 9 Weeks
Top 10 Weeks: 19
Year: 1970

81.
"Beatles '65"
The Beatles

#1 – 9 Weeks
Top 10 Weeks: 16
Year: 1965

82.
"Help!"
The Beatles/ Soundtrack

#1 – 9 Weeks
Top 10 Weeks: 15
Year: 1965

83.
"The Beatles [White Album]"
The Beatles

#1 – 9 Weeks
Top 10 Weeks: 15
Year: 1968

84.
"Pearl"
Janis Joplin

#1 – 9 Weeks
Top 10 Weeks: 15
Year: 1971

85.

"Chicago V"

Chicago

#1 – 9 Weeks
Top 10 Weeks: 13
Year: 1972

87.

"Cracked Rear View"

Hootie & The Blowfish

#1 – 8 Weeks
Top 10 Weeks: 55
Year: 1995

89.

"Slippery When Wet"

Bon Jovi

#1 – 8 Weeks
Top 10 Weeks: 46
Year: 1986

91.

"Goodbye Yellow Brick Road"

Elton John

#1 – 8 Weeks
Top 10 Weeks: 36
Year: 1973

93.
"Love Is The Thing"
Nat "King" Cole

#1 – 8 Weeks
Top 10 Weeks: 31
Year: 1957

95.
"Hotel California"
Eagles

#1 – 8 Weeks
Top 10 Weeks: 28
Year: 1977

97.
"Double Fantasy"
John Lennon/
Yoko Ono

#1 – 8 Weeks
Top 10 Weeks: 24
Year: 1980

99.
"The Hits"
Garth Brooks

#1 – 8 Weeks
Top 10 Weeks: 20
Year: 1995

THE ARTISTS

This section lists, alphabetically by artist name, every single listed in the Top 1000 ranking.

Each artist's hits are listed in rank order, with the Top 1000 ranking next to each title, along with the original label and number. This makes for a handy guide in quickly viewing each artist's all-time greatest hits.

A

AALIYAH
604 Try Again . . . . Blackground 38722

ABBA
698 Dancing Queen . . . . Atlantic 3372

ABBOTT, Gregory
693 Shake You Down . . . . Columbia 06191

ABDUL, Paula
122 Rush, Rush . . . . Virgin 98828
320 Straight Up . . . . Virgin 99256
324 Opposites Attract . . . . Virgin 99158
     Paula Abdul (with The Wild Pair)
552 Forever Your Girl . . . . Virgin 99230
701 Cold Hearted . . . . Virgin 99196
909 The Promise Of A New
     Day . . . . Captive/Virgin 98752

ACE OF BASE
57 The Sign . . . . Arista 12653
988 All That She Wants . . . . Arista 12614

ADAMS, Bryan
55 (Everything I Do) I Do It For You . A&M 1567
101 Have You Ever Really Loved
     A Woman? . . . . A&M 1028
228 All For Love . . . . A&M 0476
     Bryan Adams/Rod Stewart/Sting
560 Heaven . . . . A&M 2729

AEROSMITH
174 I Don't Want To Miss A
     Thing . . . . Columbia 78952

AGUILERA, Christina
95 Genie In A Bottle . . . . RCA Victor 65692
202 Come On Over Baby
     (all I want is you) . . . . RCA Victor 60341
497 What A Girl Wants . . . . RCA Victor 65960

A-HA
740 Take On Me . . . . Warner 29011

AIR SUPPLY
718 The One That You Love . . . . Arista 0604
970 All Out Of Love . . . . Arista 0520

ALL-4-ONE
11 I Swear . . . . Blitzz/Atlantic 87243

ALPERT, Herb
211 This Guy's In Love With You . . . . . A&M 929
421 Rise . . . . A&M 2151

AMERICA
267 A Horse With No Name . . . . Warner 7555
928 Sister Golden Hair . . . . Warner 8086

ANGELS, The
283 My Boyfriend's Back . . . . Smash 1834

ANIMALS, The
317 The House Of The Rising Sun . . MGM 13264

ANKA, Paul
177 Lonely Boy . . . . ABC-Para. 10022
354 (You're) Having My Baby . . . . United Art. 454

ARCHIES, The
618 Diana . . . . ABC-Para. 9831
156 Sugar, Sugar . . . . Calendar 1008

ARMSTRONG, Louis
614 Hello, Dolly! . . . . Kapp 573

ASSOCIATION, The
193 Windy . . . . Warner 7041
352 Cherish . . . . Valiant 747

ASTLEY, Rick
507 Never Gonna Give You Up . . RCA Victor 5347
875 Together Forever . . . . RCA Victor 8319

ATLANTIC STARR
756 Always . . . . Warner 28455

AUSTIN, Patti, with James Ingram
407 Baby, Come To Me . . . . Qwest 50036

AVALON, Frankie
116 Venus . . . . Chancellor 1031
683 Why . . . . Chancellor 1045

AWB (AVERAGE WHITE BAND)
785 Pick Up The Pieces . . . . Atlantic 3229

B

BACHMAN-TURNER OVERDRIVE
911 You Ain't Seen Nothing Yet . . . Mercury 73622

BAD ENGLISH
548 When I See You Smile . . . . Epic 69082

BANANARAMA
791 Venus . . . . London 886056

BANGLES
203 Walk Like An Egyptian . . . . . . Columbia 06257
850 Eternal Flame . . . . Columbia 68533

BARENAKED LADIES
663 One Week . . . . Reprise 17174

BASIL, Toni
632 Mickey . . . . Chrysalis 2638

BAXTER, Les
63 The Poor People Of Paris . . . . Capitol 3336
358 Unchained Melody . . . . Capitol 3055

BAY CITY ROLLERS
876 Saturday Night . . . . Arista 0149

BEACH BOYS, The
434 I Get Around . . . . Capitol 5174
532 Help Me, Rhonda . . . . Capitol 5395
803 Good Vibrations . . . . Capitol 5676
899 Kokomo . . . . Elektra 69385

BEATLES, The
23 Hey Jude . . . . Apple 2276
51 I Want To Hold Your Hand . . . . Capitol 5112
128 Get Back . . . . Apple 2490
131 Can't Buy Me Love . . . . Capitol 5150
218 Yesterday . . . . Capitol 5498
316 Hello Goodbye . . . . Capitol 2056
343 We Can Work It Out . . . . Capitol 5555

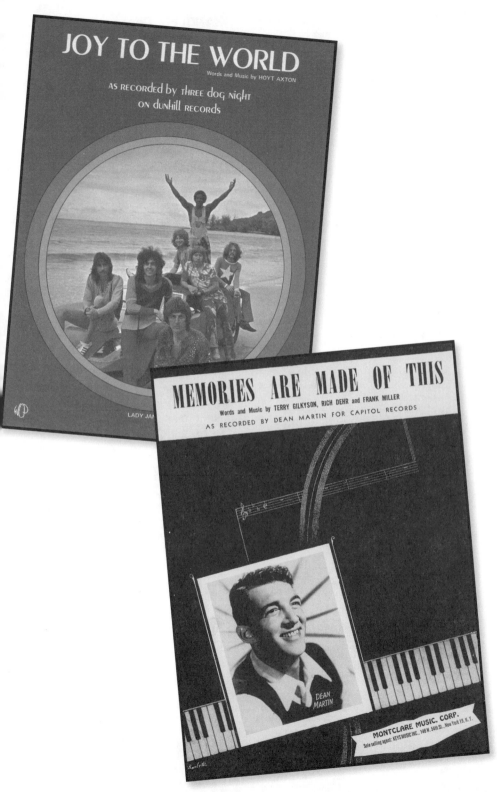

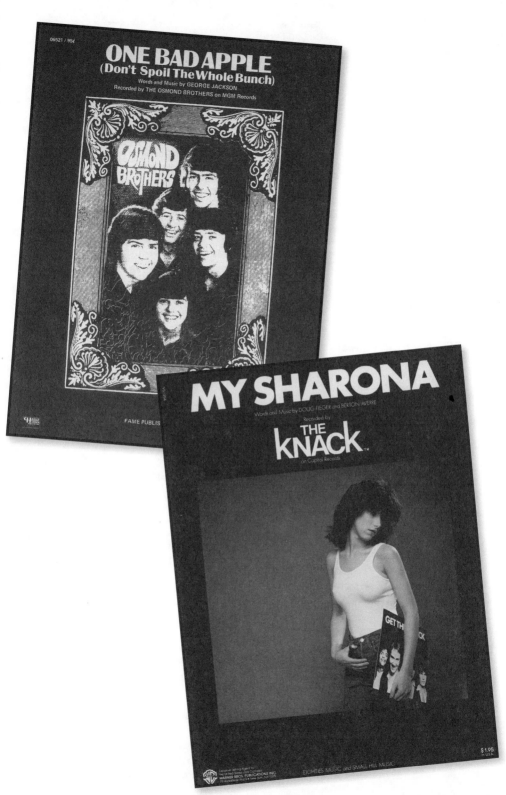

F

FABARES, Shelley
437   Johnny Angel . . . . Colpix 621

FAITH, Percy
25   The Theme From "A Summer
    Place" . . . . Columbia 41490

FALCO
333   Rock Me Amadeus . . . . A&M 2821

FENDER, Freddy
702   Before The Next Teardrop
    Falls . . . . ABC/Dot 17540

5TH DIMENSION, The
78   Aquarius/Let The Sunshine In
    (The Flesh Failures) . . . . Soul City 772
298   Wedding Bell Blues . . . . Soul City 779

FINE YOUNG CANNIBALS
754   She Drives Me Crazy . . . . . I.R.S./MCA 53483
865   Good Thing . . . . I.R.S./MCA 53639

FIREBALLS, The – see GILMER, Jimmy

FLACK, Roberta
79   The First Time Ever I Saw
    Your Face . . . . Atlantic 2864
125   Killing Me Softly With
    His Song . . . . Atlantic 2940
867   Feel Like Makin' Love . . . . Atlantic 3025

FLEETWOOD MAC
780   Dreams . . . . Warner 8371

FLEETWOODS, The
210   Come Softly To Me . . . . Dolphin 1
625   Mr. Blue . . . . Dolton 5

FONTANA, Wayne, & The Mindbenders
921   Game Of Love . . . . Fontana 1509

FONTANE SISTERS, The
229   Hearts Of Stone . . . . Dot 15265

FORD, "Tennessee" Ernie
29   Sixteen Tons . . . . Capitol 3262

FOREIGNER
456   I Want To Know What Love Is . Atlantic 89596
933   Waiting For A Girl Like You . . . . Atlantic 3868

FOUR ACES
60   Love Is A Many-Splendored
    Thing . . . . Decca 29625

FOUR LADS, The
943   Moments To Remember . . . . Columbia 40539
962   No, Not Much! . . . . Columbia 40629

4 SEASONS, The
117   Big Girls Don't Cry . . . . Vee-Jay 465
130   Sherry . . . . Vee-Jay 456
339   Walk Like A Man . . . . Vee-Jay 485
350   December, 1963 (Oh, What
    a Night) . . . . Warner/Curb 8168
537   Rag Doll . . . . Philips 40211

FOUR TOPS
406   I Can't Help Myself . . . . Motown 1076
527   Reach Out I'll Be There . . . . . . Motown 1098

FRANCIS, Connie
403   My Heart Has A Mind Of
    Its Own . . . . MGM 12923
460   Everybody's Somebody's Fool . . MGM 12899
895   Don't Break The Heart That
    Loves You . . . . MGM 13059

FRANKLIN, Aretha
525   I Knew You Were Waiting
    (For Me) . . . . Arista 9559
    Aretha Franklin And George Michael
538   Respect . . . . Atlantic 2403

FRED, John, & His Playboy Band
478   Judy In Disguise (With Glasses) . . Paula 282

FREDDIE AND THE DREAMERS
593   I'm Telling You Now . . . . Tower 125

G

GABRIEL, Peter
759   Sledgehammer . . . . Geffen 28718

GAYE, Marvin
54   I Heard It Through The
    Grapevine . . . . Tamla 54176
374   Let's Get It On . . . . Tamla 54234
670   Got To Give It Up (Pt. I) . . . . . . Tamla 54280

GAYNOR, Gloria
232   I Will Survive . . . . Polydor 14508

GEILS, J., Band
74   Centerfold . . . . EMI America 8102

GENESIS
877   Invisible Touch . . . . Atlantic 89407

GENTRY, Bobbie
194   Ode To Billie Joe . . . . Capitol 5950

GIBB, Andy
46   Shadow Dancing . . . . RSO 893
141   I Just Want To Be Your Everything. RSO 872
380   (Love Is) Thicker Than Water . . . . RSO 883

GIBBS, Georgia
224   Dance With Me Henry
    (Wallflower) . . . . Mercury 70572

GIBSON, Debbie
334   Lost In Your Eyes . . . . Atlantic 88970
846   Foolish Beat . . . . Atlantic 89109

GILDER, Nick
650   Hot Child In The City . . . . Chrysalis 2226

GILMER, Jimmy, & The Fireballs
120   Sugar Shack . . . . Dot 16487

GOLDSBORO, Bobby
121   Honey . . . . United Art. 50283

GORE, Lesley
535   It's My Party . . . . Mercury 72119

GRACIE, Charlie
476   Butterfly . . . . Cameo 105

GRAND FUNK RAILROAD
556   The Loco-Motion . . . . Capitol 3840
864   We're An American Band. . . . . . Capitol 3660

GRANT, Amy
498   Baby Baby. . . . . A&M 1549
834   The Next Time I Fall . . . . Full Moon 28597
        Peter Cetera w/Amy Grant

GRANT, Eddy
955   Electric Avenue . . . . Portrait 03793

GRANT, Gogi
28   The Wayward Wind . . . . Era 1013

GREEN, Al
672   Let's Stay Together . . . . Hi 2202

GREENE, Lorne
819   Ringo . . . . RCA Victor 8444

GUESS WHO, The
297   American Woman . . . . RCA Victor 0325

GUNS N' ROSES
508   Sweet Child O' Mine. . . . . Geffen 27963

H

HALEY, Bill, And His Comets
26   (We're Gonna) Rock Around
      The Clock . . . . Decca 29124

HALL, Daryl, & John Oates
150   Maneater. . . . . RCA Victor 13354
285   Kiss On My List. . . . . RCA Victor 12142
414   Private Eyes . . . . RCA Victor 12296
418   Out Of Touch. . . . . RCA Victor 13916
559   Rich Girl . . . . RCA Victor 10860
621   I Can't Go For That
      (No Can Do). . . . . RCA Victor 12357
973   Say It Isn't So . . . . RCA Victor 13654

HAMILTON, JOE FRANK & REYNOLDS
878   Fallin' In Love. . . . . Playboy 6024

HAMMER, Jan
773   Miami Vice Theme . . . . MCA 52666

HANSON
237   MMMBop . . . . Mercury 574261

HARRISON, George
181   My Sweet Lord . . . . Apple 2995
700   Got My Mind Set On You . . Dark Horse 28178
814   Give Me Love — (Give Me
      Peace On Earth) . . . . Apple 1862

HARRISON, Wilbert
485   Kansas City . . . . Fury 1023

HAYES, Bill
91   The Ballad Of Davy Crockett. . Cadence 1256

HAYES, Isaac
447   Theme From Shaft. . . . . Enterprise 9038

HEART
288   Alone. . . . . Capitol 44002
858   These Dreams. . . . . Capitol 5541

HEIGHTS, The
399   How Do You Talk To An Angel . Capitol 44890

HENLEY, Don – see SMYTH, Patty

HERMAN'S HERMITS
344   Mrs. Brown You've Got A
      Lovely Daughter . . . . MGM 13341
898   I'm Henry VIII, I Am . . . . MGM 13367

HI-FIVE
655   I Like The Way
      (The Kissing Game). . . . . Jive 1424

HIGHWAYMEN, The
449   Michael. . . . . United Art. 258

HILL, Faith
950   Breathe . . . . Warner 16884

HILL, Lauryn
384   Doo Wop (That Thing) . . . . . Ruffhouse 78868

HOLLY, Buddy – see CRICKETS, The

HOLLYWOOD ARGYLES
727   Alley-Oop . . . . Lute 5905

HOLMES, Rupert
258   Escape (The Piña
      Colada Song) . . . . Infinity 50,035

HONEY CONE, The
723   Want Ads. . . . . Hot Wax 7011

HORNSBY, Bruce, And The Range
699   The Way It Is . . . . RCA Victor 5023

HORTON, Johnny
72   The Battle Of New Orleans . . Columbia 41339

HOUSTON, Thelma
691   Don't Leave Me This Way . . . . . Tamla 54278

HOUSTON, Whitney
5   I Will Always Love You. . . . . . . Arista 12490
327   Greatest Love Of All . . . . Arista 9466
426   I Wanna Dance With Somebody
      (Who Loves Me) . . . . Arista 9598
503   All The Man That I Need . . . . . . Arista 2156
522   Didn't We Almost Have It All . . . . Arista 9616
545   How Will I Know . . . . Arista 9434
570   Where Do Broken Hearts Go . . . Arista 9599
605   Exhale (Shoop Shoop) . . . . . . Arista 12885
716   I'm Your Baby Tonight . . . . Arista 2108
717   So Emotional . . . . Arista 9642
745   Saving All My Love For You . . . . Arista 9381
994   Heartbreak Hotel. . . . . Arista 13619
      Whitney Houston (Feat. Faith Evans & Kelly Price)

HUES CORPORATION, The
916   Rock The Boat . . . . RCA Victor 0232

HUMAN LEAGUE, The
235   Don't You Want Me. . . . . A&M/Virgin 2397
749   Human . . . . A&M/Virgin 2861

HUNTER, Tab
73   Young Love . . . . Dot 15533

HYLAND, Brian
725   Itsy Bitsy Teenie Weenie
       Yellow Polkadot Bikini . . . . Leader 805

I

IDOL, Billy
872   Mony Mony "Live" . . . . Chrysalis 43161

IGLESIAS, Enrique
255   Be With You . . . . Interscope 490366
546   Bailamos . . . . Overbrook 97122

INGRAM, James
407   Baby, Come To Me . . . . Qwest 50036
       Patti Austin (with James Ingram)
741   I Don't Have The Heart . . . . . . Warner 19911

INXS
690   Need You Tonight . . . . Atlantic 89188

J

JACKS, Terry
287   Seasons In The Sun . . . . Bell 45,432

JACKSON, Janet
32   That's The Way Love Goes . . . . Virgin 12650
206   Miss You Much . . . . A&M 1445
236   Doesn't Really Matter . . . . . . Def Soul 562846
       Janet
293   Escapade . . . . A&M 1490
364   Again . . . . Virgin 38404
366   Together Again . . . . Virgin 38623
568   When I Think Of You . . . . A&M 2855
744   Love Will Never Do (Without You) A&M 1538
914   Black Cat . . . . A&M 1477

JACKSON, Michael
53   Billie Jean . . . . Epic 03509
56   Black Or White . . . . Epic 74100
71   Say Say Say . . . . Columbia 04168
       Paul McCartney And Michael Jackson
183   Rock With You . . . . Epic 50797
253   Beat It . . . . Epic 03759
521   Man In The Mirror . . . . Epic 07668
595   Bad . . . . Epic 07418
641   You Are Not Alone . . . . Epic 78002
808   Ben . . . . Motown 1207
862   The Way You Make Me Feel . . . . Epic 07645
873   Don't Stop 'Til You Get Enough . . Epic 50742
890   I Just Can't Stop Loving You . . . . Epic 07253
915   Dirty Diana . . . . Epic 07739

JACKSON 5
107   I'll Be There . . . . Motown 1171
445   ABC . . . . Motown 1163
446   The Love You Save . . . . Motown 1166
665   I Want You Back . . . . Motown 1157

JAMES, Sonny
616   Young Love . . . . Capitol 3602

JAMES, Tommy, And The Shondells
389   Crimson And Clover . . . . Roulette 7028
589   Hanky Panky . . . . Roulette 4686

JAN & DEAN
534   Surf City . . . . Liberty 55580

JAY-Z – see CAREY, Mariah

JEFFERSON STARSHIP – see STARSHIP

JETT, Joan, & The Blackhearts
49   I Love Rock 'N Roll . . . . Boardwalk 135

JOE – see CAREY, Mariah

JOEL, Billy
383   It's Still Rock And Roll
       To Me . . . . Columbia 11276
465   We Didn't Start The Fire . . . . Columbia 73021
751   Tell Her About It . . . . Columbia 04012

JOHN, Elton
4   Candle In The Wind 1997/
     Something About The Way
     You Look Tonight . . . . Rocket 568108
168   That's What Friends Are For . . . . Arista 9422
       Dionne & Friends
204   Don't Go Breaking My Heart . . Rocket 40585
       Elton John and Kiki Dee
275   Crocodile Rock . . . . MCA 40000
336   Island Girl . . . . MCA 40461
415   Philadelphia Freedom . . . . MCA 40364
       The Elton John Band
586   Lucy In The Sky With
     Diamonds . . . . MCA 40344
666   Bennie And The Jets . . . . MCA 40198
695   Don't Let The Sun Go
     Down On Me . . . . Columbia 74086
       George Michael/Elton John

JOHN, Robert
649   Sad Eyes . . . . EMI America 8015

JOPLIN, Janis
486   Me And Bobby McGee . . . . . Columbia 45314

JORDAN, Montell
43   This Is How We Do It . . . . . PMP/RAL 851468

JOURNEY
947   Open Arms . . . . Columbia 02687

K

KAEMPFERT, Bert
261   Wonderland By Night . . . . Decca 31141

KAMOZE, Ini
362   Here Comes The
     Hotstepper . . . . Columbia 77614

KC AND THE SUNSHINE BAND
433   That's The Way (I Like It) . . . . T.K. 1015
624   Please Don't Go . . . . T.K. 1035
626   (Shake, Shake, Shake) Shake
     Your Booty . . . . T.K. 1019
826   I'm Your Boogie Man . . . . T.K. 1022
930   Get Down Tonight . . . . T.K. 1009

LOWE, Jim
221　The Green Door. . . . . Dot 15486

LULU
123　To Sir With Love . . . . Epic 10187

L.V. – see COOLIO

M

M
648　Pop Muzik. . . . . Sire 49033

MacGREGOR, Mary
397　Torn Between Two Lovers . . . Ariola Am. 7638

MADDOX, Johnny
942　The Crazy Otto . . . . Dot 15325

MADONNA
40　Take A Bow . . . . Maverick/Sire 18000
86　Like A Virgin . . . . Sire 29210
152　Music . . . . Maverick 16826
286　Vogue . . . . Sire 19863
335　Like A Prayer. . . . . Sire 27539
479　Justify My Love . . . . Sire 19485
518　Papa Don't Preach . . . . Sire 28660
675　Crazy For You . . . . Geffen 29051
714　This Used To Be My Playground . Sire 18822
851　Open Your Heart . . . . Sire 28508
861　Live To Tell . . . . Sire 28717
888　Who's That Girl . . . . Sire 28341
969　I'll Remember. . . . . Maverick/Sire 18247

MAMAS & THE PAPAS, The
315　Monday, Monday. . . . . Dunhill 4026

MANCINI, Henry
488　Love Theme From Romeo
　　　& Juliet . . . . RCA Victor 0131

MANHATTANS, The
411　Kiss And Say Goodbye . . . . . Columbia 10310

MANILOW, Barry
638　I Write The Songs. . . . . Arista 0157
906　Looks Like We Made It . . . . Arista 0244
913　Mandy . . . . Bell 45,613

MANN, Manfred
448　Do Wah Diddy Diddy. . . . . Ascot 2157
704　Blinded By The Light. . . . . Warner 8252
　　　Manfred Mann's Earth Band

MARCELS, The
312　Blue Moon. . . . . Colpix 186

MARCH, Little Peggy
313　I Will Follow Him. . . . . RCA Victor 8139

MARKY MARK And The Funky Bunch
748　Good Vibrations. . . . . Interscope 98764

MARTIKA
566　Toy Soldiers . . . . Columbia 68747

MARTIN, Dean
66　Memories Are Made Of This . . . Capitol 3295
724　Everybody Loves Somebody . . Reprise 0281

MARTIN, Marilyn – see COLLINS, Phil

MARTIN, Ricky
99　Livin' La Vida Loca C2/Columbia 79124

MARVELETTES, The
743　Please Mr. Postman . . . . Tamla 54046

MARX, Richard
329　Right Here Waiting . . . . EMI 50219
842　Hold On To The Nights . . EMI-Manhattan 50106
910　Satisfied . . . . EMI 50189

**MASE – see NOTORIOUS B.I.G. /
　PUFF DADDY**

MASEKELA, Hugh
542　Grazing In The Grass. . . . . Uni 55066

MATCHBOX TWENTY
607　Bent. . . . . Lava 84704

MATHIS, Johnny
612　Chances Are. . . . . Columbia 40993
730　Too Much, Too Little,
　　　Too Late. . . . . Columbia 10693
　　　Johnny Mathis/Deniece Williams

MAURIAT, Paul
114　Love Is Blue. . . . . Philips 40495

McCALL, C.W.
810　Convoy . . . . MGM 14839

McCARTNEY, Paul/Wings
50　Ebony And Ivory . . . . Columbia 02860
　　　Paul McCartney (with Stevie Wonder)
71　Say Say Say . . . . Columbia 04168
　　　Paul McCartney And Michael Jackson
108　Silly Love Songs . . . . Capitol 4256
188　My Love . . . . Apple 1861
247　Coming Up (Live At
　　　Glasgow) . . . . Columbia 11263
482　With A Little Luck. . . . . Capitol 4559
782　Band On The Run. . . . . Apple 1873
805　Uncle Albert/Admiral Halsey . . . . Apple 1837
　　　Paul & Linda McCartney
812　Listen To What The Man Said . . Capitol 4091

McCOO, Marilyn, & Billy Davis, Jr.
687　You Don't Have To Be A
　　　Star (To Be In My Show) . . . . . ABC 12208

McCOY, Van
793　The Hustle. . . . . Avco 4653

McCOYS, The
815　Hang On Sloopy . . . . Bang 506

McCRAE, George
597　Rock Your Baby . . . . T.K. 1004

**McDONALD, Michael – see LaBELLE,
　Patti**

McFERRIN, Bobby
563　Don't Worry Be Happy . . EMI-Manhattan 50146

McGOVERN, Maureen
582　The Morning After. . . . . . . 20th Century 2010

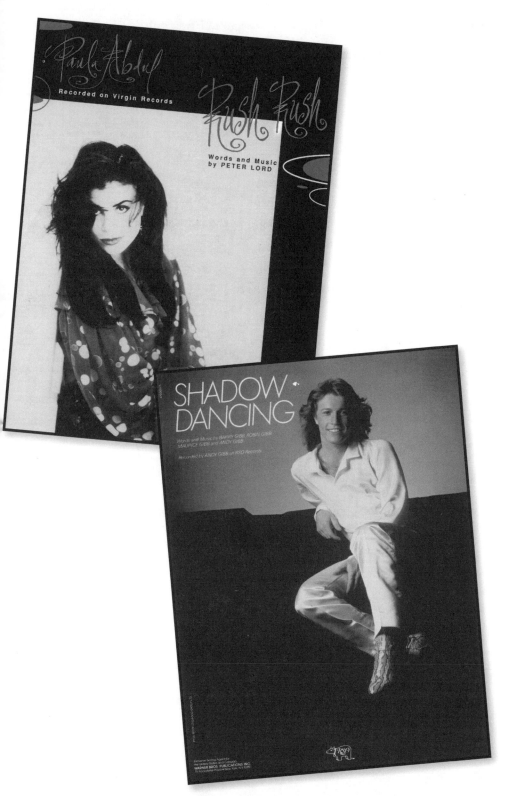

117

McGUIRE, Barry
821 Eve Of Destruction . . . . Dunhill 4009

McGUIRE SISTERS, The
16 Sincerely . . . . Coral 61323
155 Sugartime . . . . Coral 61924

McKNIGHT, Brian
937 Back At One . . . . Motown 156501

McLEAN, Don
163 American Pie - Parts I & II . . United Art. 50856

MEAT LOAF
98 I'd Do Anything For Love
(But I Won't Do That). . . . . . . MCA 54626

MECO
567 Star Wars Theme/
Cantina Band . . . . Millennium 604

MEDEIROS, Glenn, Feat. Bobby Brown
515 She Ain't Worth It . . . . MCA 53831

MEDLEY, Bill, And Jennifer Warnes
833 (I've Had) The Time Of
My Life . . . . RCA Victor 5224

MELANIE
265 Brand New Key. . . . . Neighborhood 4201

MELLENCAMP, John Cougar – see COUGAR, John

MEN AT WORK
167 Down Under . . . . Columbia 03303
652 Who Can It Be Now? . . . . . . Columbia 02888

MFSB
561 TSOP (The Sound Of
Philadelphia) . . . . Philadelphia I. 3540

MICHAEL, George/Wham!
187 Faith. . . . . Columbia 07623
270 Careless Whisper . . . . Columbia 04691
Wham! Featuring George Michael
289 Wake Me Up Before
You Go-Go. . . . . Columbia 04552
Wham!
328 One More Try . . . . Columbia 07773
525 I Knew You Were Waiting
(For Me) . . . . Arista 9559
Aretha Franklin And George Michael
558 Everything She Wants. . . . . . Columbia 04840
Wham!
572 Father Figure . . . . Columbia 07682
581 Monkey. . . . . Columbia 07941
695 Don't Let The Sun Go
Down On Me . . . . Columbia 74086
George Michael/Elton John
893 Praying For Time. . . . . Columbia 73512

MIDLER, Bette
739 Wind Beneath My Wings . . . . . Atlantic 88972

MIKE + THE MECHANICS
845 The Living Years . . . . Atlantic 88964

MILLER, Mitch
64 The Yellow Rose Of Texas. . . Columbia 40540

MILLER, Steve, Band
370 Abracadabra . . . . Capitol 5126
696 The Joker . . . . Capitol 3732
902 Rock'n Me. . . . . Capitol 4323

MILLI VANILLI
551 Blame It On The Rain. . . . . Arista 9904
553 Girl I'm Gonna Miss You . . . . . . Arista 9870
843 Baby Don't Forget My Number . . Arista 9832

MINDBENDERS, The – see FONTANA, Wayne

MIRACLES, The
404 The Tears Of A Clown . . . . Tamla 54199
824 Love Machine (Part 1). . . . . . . Tamla 54262

MR. BIG
268 To Be With You . . . . Atlantic 87580

MR. MISTER
422 Broken Wings . . . . RCA Victor 14136
516 Kyrie . . . . RCA Victor 14258

MITCHELL, Guy
17 Singing The Blues. . . . . Columbia 40769
398 Heartaches By The Number . Columbia 41476

MODUGNO, Domenico
118 Nel Blu Dipinto Di Blu (Volaré) . Decca 30677

MONICA
7 The Boy Is Mine . . . . Atlantic 84089
Brandy & Monica
90 The First Night . . . . Arista 13522
142 Angel Of Mine . . . . Arista 13590
995 Don't Take It Personal
(just one of dem days) . . . . . Rowdy 35040

MONKEES, The
52 I'm A Believer . . . . Colgems 1002
182 Daydream Believer . . . . Colgems 1012
685 Last Train To Clarksville. . . . . . Colgems 1001

MURPHY, Walter
630 A Fifth Of Beethoven . . . . . . Private S. 45,073

MURRAY, Anne
689 You Needed Me . . . . Capitol 4574

MYA
998 Case Of The Ex (Whatcha
Gonna Do) . . . . Interscope 497457

MYLES, Alannah
502 Black Velvet. . . . . Atlantic 88742

N

NASH, Johnny
205 I Can See Clearly Now . . . . Epic 10902

NELSON
753 (Can't Live Without Your)
Love And Affection . . . . DGC 19689

RIGHT SAID FRED
241   I'm Too Sexy . . . . Charisma 98671

RILEY, Jeannie C.
686   Harper Valley P.T.A. . . . . Plantation 3

RIMES, LeAnn
956   How Do I Live. . . . . Curb 73022

RIPERTON, Minnie
722   Lovin' You . . . . Epic 50057

RIVERS, Johnny
799   Poor Side Of Town . . . . Imperial 66205

ROBBINS, Marty
420   El Paso . . . . Columbia 41511

RODGERS, Jimmie
146   Honeycomb . . . . Roulette 4015

ROE, Tommy
192   Dizzy . . . . ABC 11164
583   Sheila . . . . ABC-Para. 10329

ROGERS, Kenny
70   Lady . . . . Liberty 1380
378   Islands In The Stream . . . . . RCA Victor 13615
       Kenny Rogers with Dolly Parton

ROLLING STONES, The
166   Honky Tonk Women . . . . London 910
197   (I Can't Get No) Satisfaction . . . London 9766
490   Brown Sugar. . . . . Rolling S. 19100
543   Paint It, Black. . . . . London 901
585   Get Off Of My Cloud . . . . London 9792
664   Miss You. . . . . Rolling S. 19307
787   Angie . . . . Rolling S. 19105
822   Ruby Tuesday . . . . London 904

RONSTADT, Linda
917   You're No Good. . . . . Capitol 3990

ROOFTOP SINGERS, The
536   Walk Right In . . . . Vanguard 35017

ROSE, David
680   The Stripper . . . . MGM 13064

ROSE ROYCE
674   Car Wash. . . . . MCA 40615

ROSS, Diana
24   Endless Love . . . . Motown 1519
       Diana Ross & Lionel Richie
145   Upside Down . . . . Motown 1494
280   Ain't No Mountain High
       Enough . . . . Motown 1169
429   Love Hangover. . . . . Motown 1392
694   Touch Me In The Morning. . . . . Motown 1239
786   Theme From Mahogany (Do You
       Know Where You're Going To) . Motown 1377

ROXETTE
413   It Must Have Been Love . . . . EMI 50283
779   The Look. . . . . EMI 50190
840   Listen To Your Heart . . . . EMI 50223
847   Joyride . . . . EMI 50342

ROYAL GUARDSMEN, The
981   Snoopy Vs. The Red Baron . . . . Laurie 3366

RUBY AND THE ROMANTICS
894   Our Day Will Come. . . . . Kapp 501

S

SADLER, SSgt Barry
129   The Ballad Of The Green
       Berets . . . . RCA Victor 8739

SAKAMOTO, Kyu
309   Sukiyaki . . . . Capitol 4945

SANTANA
8   Smooth . . . . Arista 13718
       Santana Feat. Rob Thomas
15   Maria Maria . . . . Arista 13773
       Santana Featuring The Product G&B

SANTO & JOHNNY
430   Sleep Walk. . . . . Canadian Amer. 103

SAVAGE GARDEN
135   I Knew I Loved You . . . . Columbia 79236
357   Truly Madly Deeply . . . . Columbia 78723

SAYER, Leo
692   You Make Me Feel Like
       Dancing. . . . . Warner 8283
761   When I Need You . . . . Warner 8332
954   More Than I Can Say . . . . . Warner 49565

SEAL
603   Kiss From A Rose . . . . ZTT/Sire 17896

SEBASTIAN, John
813   Welcome Back . . . . Reprise 1349

SEDAKA, Neil
356   Bad Blood . . . . Rocket 40460
529   Breaking Up Is Hard To Do . . RCA Victor 8046
750   Laughter In The Rain . . . . Rocket 40313

SEGER, Bob
766   Shakedown . . . . MCA 53094
979   Shame On The Moon . . . . Capitol 5187

SEMBELLO, Michael
419   Maniac . . . . Casablanca 812516

SEVILLE, David, (The Music of)
238   Witch Doctor . . . . Liberty 55132

SHAI
938   If I Ever Fall In Love . . . . Gasoline Alley 54518

SHANGRI-LAS, The
920   Leader Of The Pack . . . . Red Bird 10-014

SHANNON, Del
195   Runaway . . . . Big Top 3067

SHERIFF
904   When I'm With You . . . . Capitol 44302

SHIRELLES, The
305   Soldier Boy. . . . . Scepter 1228
505   Will You Love Me Tomorrow . . . Scepter 1211

SHOCKING BLUE, The
682   Venus . . . . Colossus 108

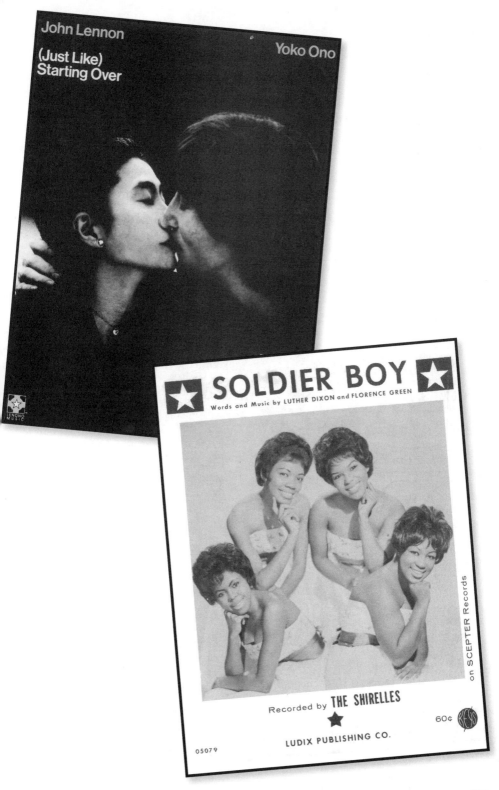

TOTO
827   Africa . . . . Columbia 03335
952   Rosanna . . . . Columbia 02811

TRAVOLTA, John, & Olivia Newton-John
657   You're The One That I Want . . . . . RSO 891

TROGGS, The
495   Wild Thing . . . . Atco 6415

TURNER, Tina
252   What's Love Got To Do With It. . Capitol 5354

TURTLES, The
281   Happy Together . . . . White Whale 244

TWAIN, Shania
934   You're Still The One . . . . Mercury 568452

TWITTY, Conway
396   It's Only Make Believe . . . . MGM 12677

2 PAC (featuring KC and JoJo)
382   How Do U Want It . . . . Death Row 854652

TYLER, Bonnie
161   Total Eclipse Of The Heart. . . Columbia 03906

TYMES, The
800   So Much In Love. . . . . Parkway 871

U

UB40
41   Can't Help Falling In Love . . . . . Virgin 12653
825   Red Red Wine. . . . . A&M 1244

USA FOR AFRICA
209   We Are The World. . . . . Columbia 04839

USHER
368   Nice & Slow . . . . LaFace 24290
941   You Make Me Wanna... . . . . . . LaFace 24265
989   My Way. . . . . LaFace 24323

U2
300   With Or Without You . . . . Island 99469
520   I Still Haven't Found What
      I'm Looking For . . . . Island 99430

V

VALLI, Frankie
461   Grease . . . . RSO 897
708   My Eyes Adored You . . . . . . Private S. 45,003

VANGELIS
668   Chariots Of Fire - Titles. . . . . . . Polydor 2189

VAN HALEN
112   Jump. . . . . Warner 29384

VANILLA ICE
746   Ice Ice Baby . . . . SBK 07335

VEE, Bobby
340   Take Good Care Of My Baby . . Liberty 55354

VERA, Billy, & The Beaters
547   At This Moment. . . . . Rhino 74403

VERNE, Larry
816   Mr. Custer. . . . . Era 3024

VERTICAL HORIZON
601   Everything You Want . . . . . . RCA Victor 65981

VILLAGE PEOPLE
999   Y.M.C.A. . . . . Casablanca 945

VINTON, Bobby
180   Roses Are Red (My Love). . . . . . . Epic 9509
199   There! I've Said It Again . . . . Epic 9638
307   Blue Velvet. . . . . Epic 9614
679   Mr. Lonely . . . . Epic 9730

W

WAITE, John
658   Missing You . . . . EMI America 8212

WARD, Anita
386   Ring My Bell. . . . . Juana 3422

WARNES, Jennifer – see MEDLEY, Bill

WARWICK, Dionne
168   That's What Friends Are For . . . . Arista 9422
      Dionne & Friends
706   Then Came You . . . . Atlantic 3202
      Dionne Warwick And the Spinners
984   (Theme From) Valley Of
      The Dolls. . . . . Scepter 12203

WATLEY, Jody
985   Looking For A New Love. . . . . . . MCA 52956

WEBER, Joan
160   Let Me Go Lover. . . . . Columbia 40366

WEISSBERG, Eric, & Steve Mandell
986   Dueling Banjos . . . . Warner 7659

WELK, Lawrence
431   Calcutta. . . . . Dot 16161

WELLS, Mary
480   My Guy . . . . Motown 1056

WHAM! – see MICHAEL, George

WHITE, Barry
931   Can't Get Enough Of Your
      Love, Babe . . . . 20th Century 2120

WHITE, Karyn
733   Romantic. . . . . Warner 19319

WHITESNAKE
752   Here I Go Again . . . . Geffen 28339

WILD CHERRY
254   Play That Funky Music . . . . Epic 50225

WILDE, Kim
857   You Keep Me Hangin' On . . . . . . MCA 53024

WILLIAMS, Andy
264 Butterfly . . . . Cadence 1308
983 Can't Get Used To
    Losing You. . . . . Columbia 42674

WILLIAMS, Deniece
424 Let's Hear It For The Boy . . . Columbia 04417
730 Too Much, Too Little,
    Too Late. . . . . Columbia 10693
    Johnny Mathis/Deniece Williams

WILLIAMS, Maurice, & The Zodiacs
903 Stay . . . . Herald 552

WILLIAMS, Roger
134 Autumn Leaves. . . . . Kapp 116

WILLIAMS, Vanessa
100 Save The Best For Last . . . . . . Wing 865136

WILL TO POWER
830 Baby, I Love Your Way/
    Freebird Medley (Free Baby) . . Epic 08034

WILSON, Al
738 Show And Tell . . . . Rocky Road 30073

WILSON PHILLIPS
504 Release Me . . . . SBK 07327
651 Hold On . . . . SBK 07322
765 You're In Love. . . . . SBK 07343

WINGS – see McCARTNEY, Paul

WINTER, Edgar, Group
763 Frankenstein. . . . . Epic 10967

WINWOOD, Steve
214 Roll With It . . . . Virgin 99326
839 Higher Love . . . . Island 28710

WITHERS, Bill
326 Lean On Me. . . . . Sussex 235

WONDER, Stevie
50 Ebony And Ivory . . . . Columbia 02860
    Paul McCartney (with Stevie Wonder)
168 That's What Friends Are For . . . . Arista 9422
    Dionne & Friends
260 I Just Called To Say I
    Love You. . . . . Motown 1745
301 Sir Duke . . . . Tamla 54281
337 Fingertips - Pt 2 . . . . Tamla 54080
707 I Wish. . . . . Tamla 54274
712 Part-Time Lover . . . . Tamla 1808
764 You Haven't Done Nothin . . . . . Tamla 54252
784 You Are The Sunshine Of
    My Life. . . . . Tamla 54232
866 Superstition. . . . . Tamla 54226

WOOLEY, Sheb
84 The Purple People Eater . . . . . . MGM 12651

WRECKX-N-EFFECT
992 Rump Shaker. . . . . MCA 54388

Y

YES
395 Owner Of A Lonely Heart . . . . . . Atco 99817

YOUNG, Neil
726 Heart Of Gold. . . . . Reprise 1065

YOUNG, Paul
697 Everytime You Go Away . . . . Columbia 04867

YOUNG RASCALS, The
126 People Got To Be Free . . . . . . Atlantic 2537
201 Groovin' . . . . Atlantic 2401
804 Good Lovin' . . . . Atlantic 2321

Z

ZAGER & EVANS
87 In The Year 2525 (Exordium
    & Terminus) . . . . RCA Victor Victor 0174

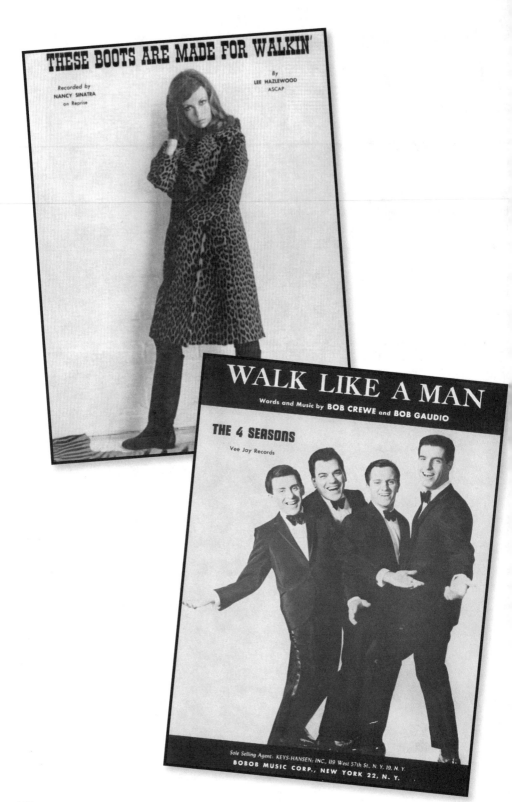

THE SONGS

This section lists, alphabetically, all titles listed in the Top 1000 ranking. Listed next to each title is its final ranking in the Top 1000.

A song with more than one charted version is listed once, with the artist's names listed below it in rank order. Songs that have the same title, but are different tunes, are listed separately, with the highest-ranked song listed first.

A

B

139

M

Y

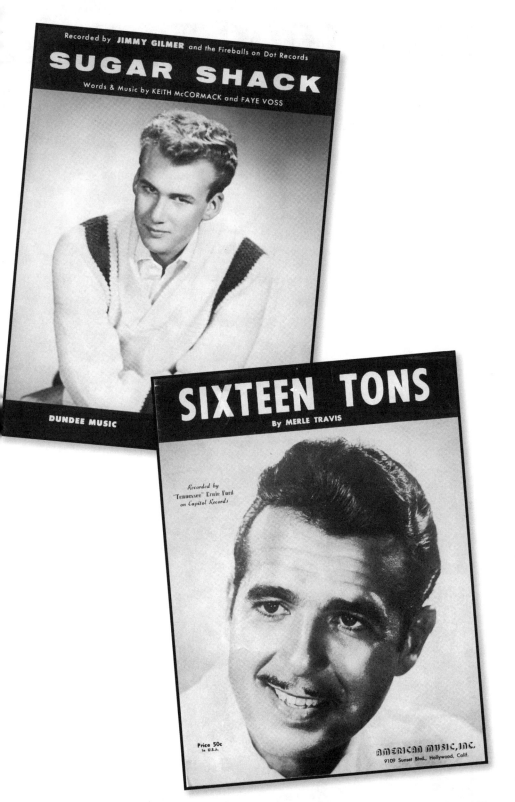

TOP 1000 TRIVIA

TOP ARTISTS

Artists with the most *Top 1000* ranked hits:

# OF HITS		
21	1.	**The Beatles**
19	2.	**Elvis Presley**
15	3.	**Mariah Carey**
13	4.	**Michael Jackson**
13	5.	**Madonna**
12	6.	**Whitney Houston**
12	7.	**The Supremes**
10	8.	**Elton John**
10	9.	**George Michael/Wham!**
10	10.	**Stevie Wonder**
9	11.	**Paul McCartney/Wings**
9	12.	**Bee Gees**
9	13.	**Janet Jackson**
8	14.	**The Rolling Stones**
7	15.	**Daryl Hall & John Oates**
7	16.	**Phil Collins**
6	17.	**Boyz II Men**
6	18.	**Pat Boone**
6	19.	**Diana Ross**
6	20.	**Paula Abdul**
5	21.	**Lionel Richie**
5	22.	**The 4 Seasons**
5	23.	**TLC**
5	24.	**Barbra Streisand**
5	25.	**Celine Dion**
5	26.	**The Everly Brothers**
5	27.	**Olivia Newton-John**
5	28.	**Prince**
5	29.	**Bon Jovi**
5	30.	**KC And The Sunshine Band**
5	31.	**Eagles**
5	32.	**John Denver**

 # OF HITS: Artist's total hits making the *Top 1000*.

or artists with the same number of *Top 1000* hits, ties are broken by totaling the final ranking of each *Top 000* hit by these artists, and the artist with the highest ranking is listed first, and so on.

SONGS WITH MORE THAN ONE HIT VERSION

Songs which charted more than one version in the *Top 1000* :

Peak Position/Year (*Top 1000* Rank)

Butterfly
Andy Williams ....1/'57 (264)
Charlie Gracie ....1/'57 (476)

Go Away Little Girl
Donny Osmond ....1/'71 (278)
Steve Lawrence ....1/'63 (443)

I'll Be There
Jackson 5..1/'70 (107)
Mariah Carey ....1/'92 (472)

Lean On Me
Bill Withers ....1/'72 (326)
Club Nouveau ....1/'87 (579)

The Loco-Motion
Grand Funk ....1/'74 (556)
Little Eva ....1/'62 (796)

Please Mr. Postman
The Marvelettes ....1/'61 (743)
Carpenters ....1/'75 (912)

Venus
The Shocking Blue....................................1/'70 (682)
Bananarama...1/'86 (791)

When A Man Loves A Woman
Percy Sledge..1/'66 (587)
Michael Bolton ....1/'91 (662)

You Keep Me Hangin' On
The Supremes ....1/'66 (588)
Kim Wilde..1/'87 (857)

Young Love
Tab Hunter ....1/'57 (73)
Sonny James ....1/'57 (616)

SAME TITLES–DIFFERENT SONGS

The following *Top 1000* songs have the same title, but are not by the same composer(s).
The artist with the highest ranked version is listed first, along with the year the title peaked:

All For Love
Bryan Adams/Rod Stewart/Sting ('94)
Color Me Badd ('92)

Best Of My Love
Emotions ('77)
The Eagles ('75)

Good Vibrations
Marky Mark & The Funky Bunch ('91)
Beach Boys ('66)

Heartbreak Hotel
Elvis Presley ('56)
Whitney Houston ('99))

Honey
Bobby Goldsboro ('68)
Mariah Carey ('97)

I'm Sorry
Brenda Lee ('60)
John Denver ('75)

Jump
Kris Kross ('92)
Van Halen ('84)

My Love
Paul McCartney & Wings ('73)
Petula Clark ('66)

One More Try
George Michael ('88)
Timmy -T- ('91)

Power Of Love
Celine Dion ('94)
Huey Lewis & The News ('85)

Venus
Frankie Avalon ('59)
The Shocking Blue ('70) and Bananarama ('86)

Wild, Wild West
Escape Club ('88)
Will Smith ('99)

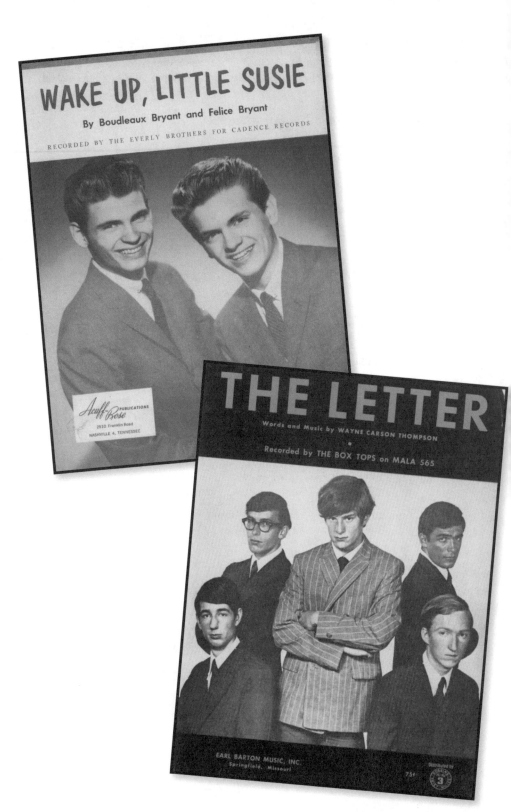

RE-CHARTED SINGLES

The *Top 1000* singles that hit the charts more than once:

BREAKDOWN BY YEAR

Total records making the *Top 1000* year-by-year:

YR	TOP 1000		YR	TOP 1000
55	17		60	22
56	20		61	21
57	24		62	20
58	24		63	22
59	15		64	24
			65	25
Total	**100** (10%)		66	28
			67	18
			68	16
			69	16
			Total	**212** (21%)

YR	TOP 1000		YR	TOP 1000
70	22		80	19
71	18		81	17
72	21		82	19
73	28		83	19
74	35		84	21
75	36		85	26
76	26		86	30
77	28		87	30
78	20		88	32
79	24		89	32
Total	**258** (26%)		**Total**	**245** (24%)

YR	TOP 1000		YR	TOP 1000
90	25		00	19
91	29			
92	18		**Total**	**19** (2%)
93	12			
94	11			
95	13			
96	11			
97	13			
98	18			
99	16			
Total	**166** (17%)			

ALL THE HITS THAT

TOP POP SINGLES 1955-1999
Over 23,000 pop singles — every "Hot 100" hit — arranged by artist. Features thousands of artist biographies and countless titles notes. Also includes the B-side title of every "Hot 100" hit. 960 pages. $79.95 Hardcover / $69.95 Softcover.

POP ANNUAL 1955-1999
A year-by-year ranking, based on chart performance, of over 23,000 pop hits. Also includes, for the first time, the songwriters for every "Hot 100" hit. 912 pages. $79.95 Hardcover / $69.95 Softcover.

POP HITS 1940-1954
Compiled strictly from *Billboard* and divided into two easy-to-use sections — one lists all the hits artist-by-artist and the other year-by-year. Filled with artist bios, title notes, and many special sections. 414 pages. Hardcover. $44.95.

POP MEMORIES 1890-1954
Unprecedented in depth and dimension. An artist-by-artist, title-by-title chronicle of the 65 formative years of recorded popular music. Fascinating facts and statistics on over 1,600 artists and 12,000 recordings, compiled directly from America's popular music charts, surveys and record listings. 660 pages. Hardcover. $59.95.

A CENTURY OF POP MUSIC
This unique book chronicles the biggest Pop hits of the past 100 years, in yearly rankings of the Top 40 songs of every year from 1900 through 1999. Includes complete artist and title sections, pictures of the top artists, top hits and top artists by decade, and more. 256 pages. Softcover. $39.95.

TOP POP ALBUMS 1955-1996
An artist-by-artist history of the over 18,300 albums that ever appeared on *Billboard* 's Pop albums charts, with a complete A-Z listing below each artist of *every* track from *every* charted album by that artist. 1,056 pages. Hardcover. $89.95.

TOP POP ALBUM TRACKS 1955-1992
An all-inclusive, alphabetical index of every song track from every charted music album, with the artist's name and the album's chart debut year. 544 pages. Hardcover. $34.95.

TOP POP ALBUM TRACKS 1993-1996
A 3 1/2-year supplement to the above Tracks book — alphabetically indexes over 21,000 tracks from the more than 1,600 albums that have appeared on *The Billboard 200* Pop Albums charts since 1992. 88 pages. Softcover. $14.95.

BILLBOARD HOT 100/POP SINGLES CHARTS: collections of the actual weekly "Hot 100" charts from each decade;
THE NINETIES 1990-1999 — black-and-white reproductions at 70% of original size. Over 550 pages each.
THE EIGHTIES 1980-1989 — Deluxe hardcover. $79.95 each.
THE SEVENTIES 1970-1979
THE SIXTIES 1960-1969

POP CHARTS 1955-1959 — Reproductions of every weekly Pop singles chart *Billboard* published from 1955 through 1959 ("Best Sellers," "Jockeys," "Juke Box," "Top 100" and "Hot 100"). 496 pages. Deluxe hardcover. $59.95.

BILLBOARD POP ALBUM CHARTS 1965-1969
The greatest of all album eras...straight off the pages of *Billboard* ! Every weekly *Billboard* Pop albums chart, from 1965 through 1969. Black-and-white reproductions at 70% of original size. 496 pages. Deluxe hardcover. $59.95.

BUBBLING UNDER SINGLES AND ALBUMS 1998 Edition
All "Bubbling Under The Hot 100" (1959-1997) and "Bubbling Under The Top Pop Albums" (1970-1985) charts covered in full and organized artist by artist. Also features a photo section of every EP that hit *Billboard's* "Best Selling Pop EP's" chart (1957-1960). 416 pages. Softcover. $49.95.

TOP COUNTRY SINGLES 1944-1997
The complete history of the most genuine of American musical genres, with an artist-by-artist listing of every "Country" single ever charted. 544 pages. Hardcover. $64.95.

COUNTRY ANNUAL 1944-1997
A year-by-year ranking, based on chart performance, of over 16,000 Country hits. 704 pages. Hardcover. $64.95.

TOP COUNTRY ALBUMS 1964-1997
First edition! A music industry first and a Record Research exclusive — features an artist-by-artist listing of every album to appear on *Billboard's* Top Country Albums chart from its first appearance in 1964 through September, 1997. Includes

EVER CHARTED

TOP R&B SINGLES 1942-1999
Revised edition of our R&B bestseller — loaded with new features! Every "Soul," "Black," "Urban Contemporary" and "Rhythm & Blues" charted single, listed by artist. 688 pages. Hardcover. $69.95.

TOP R&B ALBUMS 1965-1998
First edition! An artist-by-artist listing of each of the 2,177 artists and 6,940 albums to appear on *Billboard's* "Top R&B Albums" chart. Includes complete listings of all tracks from every Top 10 R&B album. 360 pages. Hardcover. $49.95.

BILLBOARD TOP 10 SINGLES CHARTS 1955-2000
A complete listing of each weekly Top 10 chart, along with each week's "Highest Debut" and "Biggest Mover" from the entire "Hot 100" chart, and more! Over 650 pages. Softcover. $49.95.

BILLBOARD TOP 10 ALBUM CHARTS 1963-1998
This books contains more than 1,800 individual Top 10 charts from over 35 years of *Billboard's* weekly Top Albums chart (currently titled The Billboard 200). 536 pages. Hardcover. $39.95.

TOP ADULT CONTEMPORARY 1961-1993
America's leading listener format is covered hit by hit in this fact-packed volume. Lists, artist by artist, the complete history of *Billboard's* "Easy Listening" and "Adult Contemporary" charts. 368 pages. Hardcover. $39.95.

ROCK TRACKS
Two artist-by-artist listings of the over 3,700 titles that appeared on *Billboard's* "Album Rock Tracks" chart from March, 1981 through August, 1995 and the over 1,200 titles that appeared on *Billboard's* "Modern Rock Tracks" chart from September, 1988 through August, 1995. 288 pages. Softcover. $34.95.

BILLBOARD TOP 1000 x 5 1996 Edition
Includes five complete *separate* rankings — from #1 through #1000 — of the all-time top charted hits of Pop & Hot 100 Singles 1955-1996, Pop Singles 1940-1954, Adult Contemporary Singles 1961-1996, R&B Singles 1942-1996, and Country Singles 1944-1996. 288 pages. Softcover. $29.95.

BILLBOARD SINGLES REVIEWS 1958
Reproductions of every weekly 1958 record review *Billboard* published for 1958. Reviews of nearly 10,000 record sides by 3,465 artists. 280 pages. Softcover. $29.95.

DAILY #1 HITS 1940-1992
A desktop calendar of #1 pop records. Lists one day of the year per page of every record that held the #1 position on the Pop singles charts on that day for each of the past 53+ years. 392 pages. Spiral-bound softcover. $24.95.

BILLBOARD #1s 1950-1991
A week-by-week listing of every #1 *single* and *album* from *Billboard's* Pop, R&B, Country and Adult Contemporary charts. 336 pages. Softcover. $24.95.

MUSIC YEARBOOKS 2000/1999/1998/1997/1996/1995/1994/1993/1992/1991/1990
A complete review of each year's charted music — as well as a superb supplemental update of our Record Research Pop Singles and Albums, Country Singles, R&B Singles, Adult Contemporary Singles, and Bubbling Under Singles books. Various page lengths. Softcover. 2000 & 1999 edition $39.95 / 1995 thru 1998 editions $34.95 each / 1990 thru 1994 editions $29.95 each.

For complete book descriptions and ordering/shipping rate information, call, write, fax or e-mail today.

RECORD RESEARCH INC.
P.O. Box 200
Menomonee Falls, WI 53052-0200   U.S.A.
Phone: 262/251-5408 / Fax: 262/251-9452
E-mail: books@recordresearch.com

We're On The Internet — If you'd like to place an order electronically, simply use the convenient order form on our Web Site: **www.recordresearch.com**.

JOEL WHITBURN:
CHARTING HIS OWN COURSE

From pastime to passion to profitable enterprise, the growth of Record Research has been the outgrowth of Joel Whitburn's hobby. Joel began collecting records as a teenager in the 1950s. As his collection grew, he began to sort, categorize and file each record according to the highest position it reached on *Billboard's* Hot 100 charts. He went on to publish this information in 1970 and a business was born.

Today, Joel leads a team of researchers who delve into all of *Billboard's* music and video charts with an unmatched degree of depth and detail. Widely recognized as the most authoritative historian on charted music, Joel has also collaborated with Rhino Records on a series of over 145 CD compilations of America's top charted hits. Joel's own record collection remains unrivaled the world over and includes every charted Hot 100 and pop single (back to 1920), every charted pop album (back to 1945), collections of nearly every charted Country, R&B, Bubbling Under The Hot 100 and Adult Contemporary records, and every video to chart since *Billboard* began its video charts in 1979. Ever the consummate collector, Joel also owns one of the world's largest picture sleeve collections, many of which he displays in the series of books (*Top 40 Hits, Top 40 Albums, Top 40 Country Hits*) he writes for *Billboard's* book division.

In person, this walking music encyclopedia stands 6'6" — a definite advantage when he played high school, college and semi-pro basketball. An avid sports fan, Joel actively engages in a wide variety of water, winter and motor sports. A native of Wisconsin, Joel has been married for 37 years to Fran, a native of Honduras; their daughter, Kim Bloxdorf, is part of the Record Research team, as are two of Joel's friends and key employees of 31 years, Bill Hathaway and Brent Olynick. Joel's lifelong passion for music, old and new, and his penchant for accurate detail continues into the 21st century.